WEALTH M

WEALTH MANAGEMENT

How not to throw away your riches

KEVIN QUINN

BLACKHALL
Publishing

This book was typeset by Ark Imaging for

Blackhall Publishing
33 Carysfort Avenue
Blackrock
Co. Dublin
Ireland

e-mail: info@blackhallpublishing.com
www.blackhallpublishing.com

© Kevin Quinn, 2007

ISBN (HBK): 978 1 84218 128 7
ISBN (PBK): 978 1 84218 117 1

A catalogue record for this book is available from the British Library.

All rights reserved. No part of this publication may be reproduced, stored in a retrieval system or transmitted in any form or by any means, electronic, mechanical, photocopying, recording or otherwise, without the prior, written permission of the publisher.

This book is sold subject to the condition that it shall not, by way of trade or otherwise, be lent, resold, hired out, or otherwise circulated without the publisher's prior consent in any form of binding or cover other than that in which it is published and without a similar condition including this condition being imposed on the subsequent purchaser.

Printed in the UK by Athenaeum Press Ltd

About the Author

Kevin Quinn is an associate director at Bank of Ireland Private Banking, working in areas that include product development, investments, pensions, and marketing. He has been working in the Irish financial services sector for seventeen years and has been a member of Private Banking's executive team since 2000. Prior to this, he held a variety of product and marketing roles in Bank of Ireland Asset Management and in Irish Life's life assurance, investment management and home loan companies.

Kevin is a business graduate of Trinity College Dublin and holds a Masters degree in Investment and Treasury Management from Dublin City University. He is an associate of the Society of Investment Analysts in Ireland, a member of the CFA© Institute and a member of the Marketing Institute of Ireland. He was co-author of *Investment Advice for Life*, first published in 1998.

To Isabelle

Contents

Preface ix

Acknowledgements xi

PART I: MAKING SENSE OF THE CAPITAL MARKETS 1

1. **Introduction: Humpty Dumpty and Professor Markowitz** 3

    1.1 The Big Pieces – Equities, Property, Bonds, Hedge Funds, Private Equity and Commodities 4

    1.2 Putting Humpty Dumpty back together again 16

2. **Resetting your Expectations from 2007 Onwards** 19

    2.1 From 2007 Onwards – Through the Looking Glass 19

    2.2 The Building Blocks of Financial Asset Returns 20

    2.3 Know your OATs 23

    2.4 Equities – The Incredible Shrinking Equity Risk Premium 24

    2.5 Property – The World's Greatest Asset Class or Smoke and Mirrors? 44

    2.6 Bonds – Europe and the US, a Tale of Two Continents 66

    2.7 Private Equity – The New Kings of Capitalism 76

Contents

    2.8   Commodities – The Building Blocks
of New Economies 83

    2.9   Hedge Funds – The New Kid in Town 87

    2.10 Asset Class Almanac 2007 106

PART TWO: PUTTING YOUR PLANS IN PLACE 121

3. Asset Pools and Acronyms **123**

    3.1   Tax Treatments of Assets in Personal
and Business Structures 123

    3.2   Investment and Taxation for Business Owners ... 127

    3.3   The Case for Personal Pensions, Executive Pensions, Company Pensions, AVCs, Annuities, ARFs, SSAPs and PRSAs 130

4. Personal Wealth Protection for Business Owners ... **145**

    4.1   A Reminder to put the CAT out 145

    4.2   Preparing Personal and Corporate Wills 153

    4.3   Protecting your Family and your Business ... 155

    4.4   Using Debt as a Tool in your Financial Planning ... 162

A Word about Advisors **169**

    Bibliography 173

    Index 179

PREFACE

This is not a book about how to 'get rich quick'. Most such books, in my view, are the produce of lucky breaks or megalomaniac charlatans. There is no way to 'make a million in year' without having a lot of luck, hard work or skill on your side – or indeed having ten million with which to start the year. Regrettably neither is there a secret black box lurking in the private banks, investment banks or stockbroking firms of the world.

Rather this is a book about what to do next – how to keep your personal wealth growing, what your options are, how to protect it from some of the risks you've probably ignored until now and, ultimately, how to plan to ensure your wealth is there for future generations.

The book is aimed at successful business owners who have sweated on the way to riches; people who work six and seven days a week, year after year, to start businesses and then worry about how to keep them profitable; people who often take unusually high personal financial risks, and don't pay attention to the risks they have taken; people who know better than I how to run businesses and turn dreams into financial success.

In writing a book of this kind it was necessary to 'dip into' disciplines as diverse as investment portfolio theory, economics, tax, pensions, life assurance and law. I am not an expert in all and in so doing I have borrowed from many recent academic and professional works in an effort to make this material accessible to today's business owner. By its nature a book such as this can only glance off each of these subjects and, at times, the abbreviation does little to reflect the depth of each subject.

Acknowledgements

I would like to thank a number of my colleagues on whose greater expertise I depended on for a number of areas, in particular Declan Lawlor, for the significant sections he contributed on pensions and business protection; Dennis Slattery, on whose original work I based much of the hedge fund material; Judy Nally, who reviewed the tax-related areas, and Pat O'Sullivan. My thanks also to Mark Cunningham for his valued critique. I am most grateful to each for their individual contributions and criticisms. Most particularly, I am grateful to my employers, Bank of Ireland Private Banking, for the opportunities to work in and learn about so many diverse areas of personal finance.

I would also like to say a word of thanks to Gerard O'Connor of Blackhall Publishing, for his encouragement and good humour throughout this book's long gestation and to my life-long friend Cormac Hanley, one of Ireland's most talented photographers, for his work on the book cover. My thanks also to Elizabeth Brennan who guided me through the process of editing.

Above all my thanks and love to my wife Isabelle, for her love and support and for the many Saturday afternoons, holidays and late evenings spent writing this book that I should have spent with her.

I am grateful to all for their assistance in making this book possible – all blame for errors, inaccuracies and opinions that prove to be wrong lies with me.

Kevin Quinn
Dublin, December 2006

Part I

Making Sense of the Capital Markets

CHAPTER 1

Introduction: Humpty Dumpty and Professor Markowitz

From my earliest encounters with investors I was struck by the obvious trade-off that puzzles so many people – risk versus return. Even in conversations with the wealthiest of individuals, they too often begin with, 'I'd like to make a decent return on my money, better than deposit', to be quickly followed by, 'but be sure not to lose any of my money; I'm not too keen on putting capital at risk.'

It is an understandable instinct to want to protect one's hard-earned wealth, an instinct that is hardwired into our psychology. And it's not one that changes the wealthier one becomes. Yet it is the root cause of the fuzzy thinking that is one of the greater impediments to reaching a sensibly managed portfolio. It is hardly surprising that most investors end up with a portfolio that matches their levels of comfort and understanding, as opposed to matching their desired outcomes and objectives or even making financial sense. Not that this is a bad thing, but the consequence can be portfolios where a house in every county in Ireland represents 'well diversified' or a deposit account with every bank is 'spreading the risk around'.

If either of those characterisations sound familiar, don't worry, you are in good company. You are among the vast majority of people, wealthy and otherwise, for whom 'asset allocation' probably means little more than 'not putting all your eggs in one basket'. The principle is sound. Yet, for most people, translating this adage into an investment portfolio is a foreign country.

The academic lexicon of asset allocation was created by the work of Professor Markowitz in the early 1950s and has been finding its way into the conventions of investment advice ever since. Finding the right way to put the pieces back together again – to fit the various assets together in a way that minimises risks and gets the best risk-adjusted return – has been the pursuit of financial planners across the globe. Most have pursued Markowitz's theories in some manner – unwitting slaves of an economist from an earlier time.

1.1. The Big Pieces – Equities, Property, Bonds, Hedge Funds, Private Equity and Commodities

Let's begin at the beginning. There are four asset classes: equities, bonds, cash and property. This is what every financial advisor learns in investments 1.01 and it's in need of an update; or at least it's an abbreviated version of what the investment industry can now offer for your portfolio.

The pool of assets is the full range of assets that can be bought or sold in the pursuit of your objectives. It includes the four main asset classes but also stretches to include the more esoteric parts of the capital markets including the various forms of alternative investing (e.g. hedge funds, private equity, commodities and managed futures) and the less well-priced, illiquid real asset categories including art and collectibles. It also stretches beyond buying an asset, holding it and then selling it. It should include the various techniques that are available to the professional investor – particularly the use of debt to finance investments, but the use of methods such as 'shorting', 'hedging' and other techniques as well. By combining the full range of asset classes with the various techniques, investors are armed with a full appreciation of what the professionals can do.

Equities and the Long Run

Most financial advisors begin with the principal that 'stocks win in the long run'. Historically this has proven to be one of the more reliable planks upon which financial plans are built and it has been a source of colossal wealth creation for investors – more than anything else in modern capital market history. This 'cult of the equity' is built on a compellingly simple principle that has strong – indeed indisputable – evidence from economic history. The principle is that once one survives the volatility that the stock market inevitably presents in the short term one will be compensated by periods of incredible returns that, in the long run, would deliver a better average return than other assets.

Professor Jeremy Siegel's *Stocks for the Long Run*[1] is the Bible, or at least the user's manual, of the equity cult and presents an impossibly articulate case for equities being the dominant part of any portfolio. I would recommend that any serious investor take the time to read this, as it is certainly the best primer on stock market investing. Its findings are backed, in a less US-centric form, in *Triumph of the Optimists* by Elroy Dimson et al.[2] – a more

1.1. The Big Pieces

recently published analysis of the returns from international capital markets over the past century from a host of different countries. All of the evidence points to one unassailable fact: equities beat other assets spectacularly and persistently in the past century, when judged from the perspective of the start of the twenty-first century. In short, there is simply a plethora of evidence available to support the precept that equities should be a dominant part of a portfolio. It is a principle best encapsulated in Figure 1.1, a chart taken from Professors Siegel's book.

At first glance, this chart presents a killer argument. A single US dollar invested in the stock market would have delivered $8.8m by 2001; no mean achievement by comparison to the performance of gold which appreciated to a mere $14.67. Even allowing for the fact that the analysis is US based and therefore reflects the growth of a country from colonial wilderness to the dominant economic power on the planet, and if one knocks off a few per cent for the impact of investors not choosing the right stocks or spending the dividends (a huge contributor to the long-term returns being

Figure 1.1: Total Nominal Return Indices 1802–2001 (Value of $1 invested in 1802)

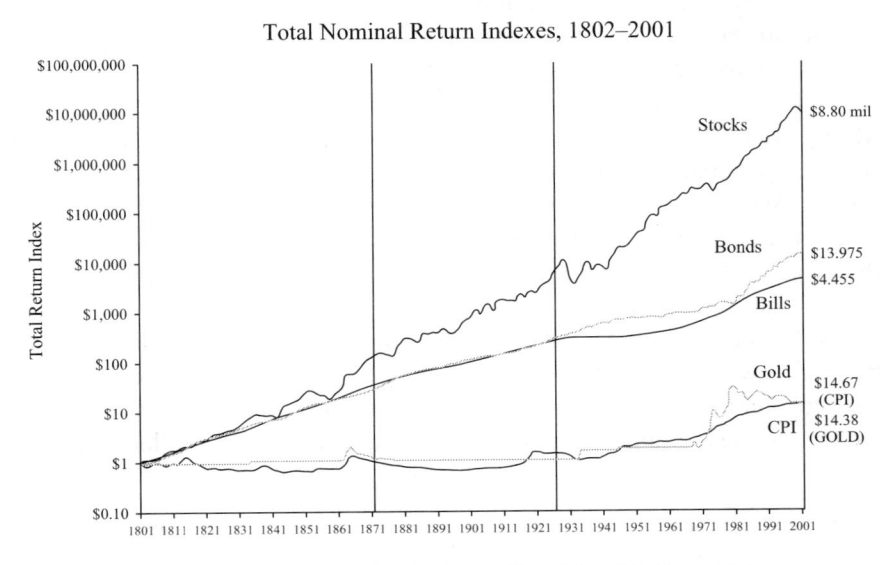

Source: J. Siegal (2002), *Stocks for the Long Run*, UK: McGraw Hill. Reproduced with the kind permission of Professor Jeremy Siegel.

so impressive), it still sits head and shoulders above other investments. If it were so unequivocally correct that equities always win out in the long run the simple logic should be that everyone should invest in equity. A charmingly appealing statistic, it unintentionally serves to disprove its own argument – the idea that stocks are ever held for such long periods is simply untrue as no single family kept hold of that dollar, reinvested it and chose firms that survived and kept pace with the market for two centuries.

Yet the 'cult of the equity', which holds as its unassailable truth the fact that equities have always beaten other assets, has faced one of its more challenging periods since the bear market* of 2000–2003. Investors, most importantly institutional investors, had begun to hold equities in greater amounts in the decade preceding the crash and they were richly rewarded over a two decade bull run† of extraordinary strength. Evidence of the increasing sway held by the rising equity market can be seen in the rise in average allocation to equities by US pension funds which increased from circa 40 per cent to between 65 per cent and 75 per cent by the late 1990s. Then along came 2000–2003, uninvited by real recession, more a product of an irrationally priced market and humbled market professionals.

This was despite the fact that the bull market of 1982–2000, in which double digit returns from equities became the norm, was peppered by short-term setbacks: the 1987 crash; the downturn caused by the First Gulf War; the turbulence in 1994 as the US hiked interest rates and again in 1997–1998 with the Far East currency crisis; the Long Term Capital Management (LTCM) hedge fund crisis; and the collapse of the Russian Rouble, culminating in the heady days of the late 1990s with the technology bubble. Where previous crises proved transitory in the face of the rising stock market, the bear market saw equities destroy wealth in the ensuing three years on a grand scale. However, in reality, this wealth could never be realised, it was simply mispriced.

The bubble in equities in the late 1990s deflated in a healthy fashion and by 2003 it was ripe to rebound, which it did handsomely. However, its three year rebound did little to persuade long-term bears that the equity market would ever be the same again. Influential academic Robert Shiller famously

---

* 'Bear market' refers to a period of falling prices and pessimism about the future trend in prices.

† 'Bull run' refers to a period of rising prices and optimism about the future trend in prices.

1.1. The Big Pieces

Figure 1.2: The Disconnection between Earnings and Prices in the Stock Market, 1870–2005

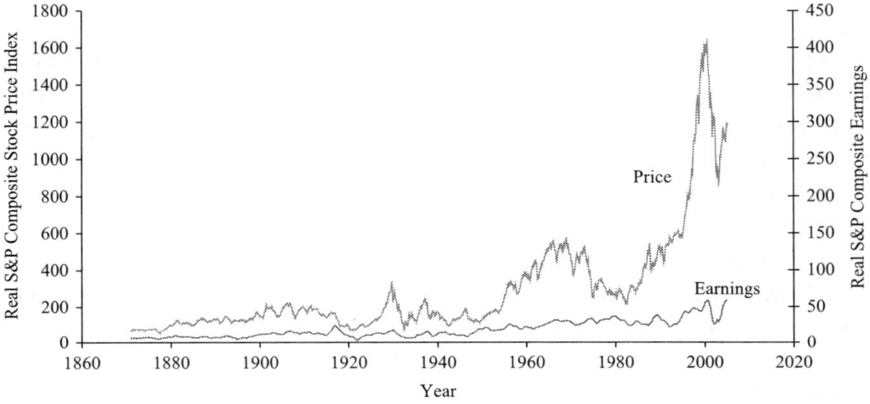

Source: SHILLER, ROBERT J.; *IRRATIONAL EXHUBERANCE*. © 2000 Robert J. Shiller, published by Princeton University Press. Reprinted by permission of Princeton University Press.

critiqued stock market overvaluation in 2000 in his (in)famous publication *Irrational Exuberance*[3] and his assertions have since proven prescient. (His recently published second edition (April 2005) suggests property is now the bubbling asset – which might give some pause for thought.) As a counter balance to the optimism of others, this too should feature on any well-informed investor's reading list. His arguments are a most convincing counter-balance to anyone who believes that the double digit returns of the past two decades can repeat, by simply highlighting the extent to which equities have become much more expensive. Figure 1.2 from *Irrational Exuberance* illustrates this, graphically depicting the extent to which equity prices departed from earnings in particular in the late 1990s.

As an investor you should cast your mind back to 1982 at the start of the last secular bull run in equities when bond yields were in the mid teens, dividend yields were about 6–7 per cent and P/E's* were on average about

---

*P/E stands for 'Price/Earnings ratio', a commonly used measure of valuation of shares. The measure indicates the number of euros an investor must pay for one euro of company earnings, so a P/E of 15 means investors must pay €15 for €1 in company earnings. It is also referred to as 'earnings multiple'.

nine times earnings. It was bargain basement by comparison to nowadays (although optimists could rightly argue that earnings multiples in mid 2006 were at their cheapest level in a decade). Figure 1.3 illustrates the extent to which valuations had been stretched.

What we face, therefore, is an asset that has convinced a generation or perhaps two generations that it is largely infallible in the long run but that, at the same time, has managed to become more expensive than its historic norms by most measures. Economist Paul Samuelson put it succinctly in suggesting that the stock market was 'micro-efficient' and 'macro-inefficient' – great at pricing individual stocks but not so good at the bigger picture. In other words, the market may be right in the short term but missing the bigger picture relative to where it has come from. The same may also apply to property markets. An equally powerful point was made by Benjamin Graham in his oft quoted remark that the stock market is a voting machine in the short run and a weighing machine in the long run.[4] Put simply, the market will depend on sentiment in the near term but, in the longer run, fundamentals tend to have a magnet-like effect that can humble even the most ardent believer in new paradigms.

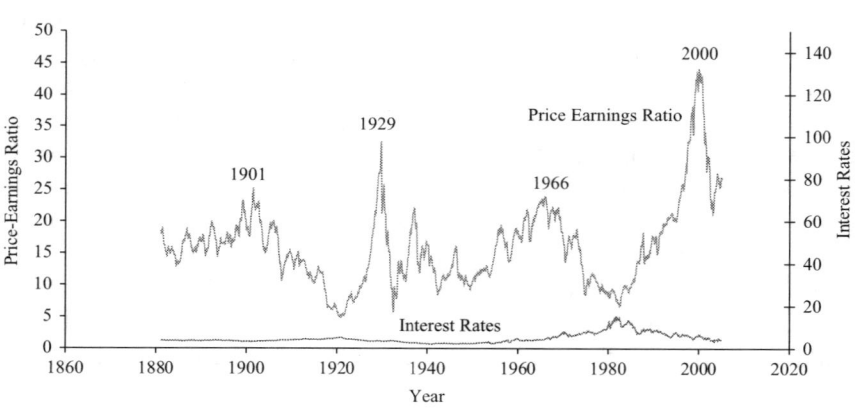

Figure 1.3: The Long-Term Price-Earnings Ratio, 1880–2005

Source: SHILLER, ROBERT J.; *IRRATIONAL EXHUBERANCE*. © 2000 Robert J. Shiller, published by Princeton University Press. Reprinted by permission of Princeton University Press.

1.1. The Big Pieces

Putting a Measure on the Future

The way financial economists attempt to capture and measure this looking forward is the 'equity risk premium' – the measure of the amount by which investors must be compensated over and above fixed-interest investing to take on the risk of the stock market. In some ways this is the most important and yet elusive of measures and hence I have devoted a substantial section to it in Chapter 2. Suffice to say at this stage that my belief is that equities should continue to be a core part of most business owners' portfolios but the return will be much more muted than it has been historically with the equity risk premium for the coming generation being closer to 2–3 per cent. This creates many issues, on which I will expand in Section 2.2 of Chapter 2.

Property's Infallibility

For Irish investors, the property market has been a one-way bet for a generation. Its rise has been almost unparalleled (quite literally across global capital markets) and it has fuelled a growth in wealth in the country of a kind that we have never seen before.

Whatever the root cause of the dramatic increase in property prices (and I would point to one main culprit: the shift to significantly lower interest rates), property has been the investment of choice for Irish investors for the past decade. Witness the over €11 billion in (leveraged) Irish capital that flowed from Irish pockets into bricks and mortar in 2006 alone (of which only €3 billion was invested in Ireland). As can be seen from Table 1.1 the popularity of property investment has been rewarded handsomely.

Of course the usual suspects are lined up for medals in most histories of the Celtic Tiger period: interest rates fell from the late teens/early twenties to low single digits; a young population swelled into the child-bearing years and, coupled with immigration, gave us a demography like nothing else in Europe; relatively low incomes to begin with and reasonable standards of education coupled with the English language and, God bless it, the triple-gold-medal-winning low tax system. With hindsight, there should be no prizes for guessing what would happen to property.

It hasn't all been rosy. While the housing market continued to simmer nicely, the twin cracks of rising vacancies and falling rents caused

Table 1.1: Total Returns from Irish Property by Sector

	Retail	Office	Industrial
1984	−4.5	−0.1	1.4
1985	−1.9	−0.1	3.7
1986	9.4	5.3	5.1
1987	17.2	6.9	13.8
1988	22.8	15.6	21.1
1989	35.5	35.8	42.3
1990	9.2	12.5	21.6
1991	0.9	−1.6	4.0
1992	−0.4	−3.5	3.0
1993	9.4	4.8	12.3
1994	16.4	14.4	21.5
1995	14.1	12.1	15.3
1996	18.3	19.5	21.0
1997	23.3	26.5	25.9
1998	34.1	43.3	29.0
1999	22.4	36.5	28.1
2000	24.6	31.4	23.5
2001	10.8	6.8	9.1
2002	13.0	−2.4	1.0
2003	26.9	6.2	6.7
2004	7.2	2.7	2.8
2005	27.4	23.7	16.2
2006*	26.7	27.6	25.4

* 12 months to end September 2006
Source: Investment Property Databank, Annual Index 2006, <http://www.ipdindex.co.uk/results/indices/ireland/index_ireland.asp>, accessed 2/2/2007.

investors to wince in the post-Tiger slowing of 2001–2002. Not for long however, as 2003–2006 produced another bumper crop of returns in most sectors.

It seems the economic moat that surrounds the Republic of Ireland has been shored up again. But will it last? Relative valuations arguments are once again stalking the market with reduced rental yields making the sums more demanding for would-be investors in local residential property.

Of course the appeal of property lies as much in its returns (which have been behind equities over most periods) as in the extent to which banks

1.1. The Big Pieces

are prepared to lend against bricks and mortar. Putting a bank's capital at risk, for most investors, is a far less challenging part of the investment equation and borrowing has been the catalyst for an immense growth in investment values in recent times.

At the heart of property's popularity are features that distinguish it from other assets. It rests at the top of the scale when it comes to opaque pricing. With highly illiquid and almost completely unique characteristics applying to most commercial property investments, its clunky price movements make for much greater apparent stability than its equity cousin. Add in a dose of low interest financed gearing and, in particular, a falling interest rate environment and *Alakazam*, you get double digit returns.

Property prices don't fall? Of course they do. Speculative bubbles can and do happen in the property market also. For property's equivalent to the 1929 Wall Street Crash, consider Florida after the First World War.[5] Having become a popular holiday and retirement destination, demand soared causing prices to double and triple (in a justifiable fashion). The gains brought speculation, to a point where prices reached untenable levels – by 1926 it cost $4.5m (unadjusted for inflation!) to buy a luxury gate guarded home in Miami, much the same as it does today. There are other examples scattered across the globe – New England, London, Tokyo (which, if sold at its peak, would have generated enough capital to buy all property in the US!) to name but a few.

However, it is comforting to know that property price crashes are a far less frequent occurrence and generally less deep than their equity cousin. A recent IMF* paper suggested that you can expect a property crash about every twenty years compared to an equity crash every thirteen years.[6] What's more, they tend to be somewhat less severe in magnitude – although their long-term economic consequences can make just as great an impact.

Nonetheless, based on recent evidence at least, what we face with property is an asset that can more justifiably claim infallibility, or at least a more imperfect pricing mechanism that is less prone to correction.

Bonds

Bonds are negotiable promissory notes issued by a government or a corporate body. The par value is the price at which it is issued – typically

---
* International Monetary Fund

it is also the amount that the issuer promises to pay at maturity. The coupon is the amount that the issuer promises to pay periodically.

Then there's the price at which it trades – the market price. Buffeted by interest rate risk, credit risk and sentiment about the Fed or the European Central Bank's (ECB) next move, the market price is usually a slightly less predictable animal. Measured better in terms of 'yield to maturity' and 'duration', the bond market presents a mystery to most first time investors. Nonetheless, with greater predictability in the cash flows than its sister equity, finding the price of a bond at any one point in time is generally a less hazardous occupation, albeit one suited to your average Ph.D. maths student. Any way you look at it the bond market is one of the most important elements in the world of finance worth a mesmerising $45 trillion+ in assets. Bonds are a colossal part of the wider capital markets world – four to five times bigger than the value of the investable property market – and form a part of everyone's portfolio in some shape or fashion, whether consciously or otherwise. Bonds have also enjoyed a period of relatively healthy returns over the past two decades as they too enjoyed the benefits of the long-term downward trend in interest rates.

Hedge Funds

Mention these words in hushed tones: Long-term Capital Management, George Soros, Tiger, breaking the Bank of England. These are the first thoughts that cross the minds of many investors when faced with what Peter Temple eloquently described as 'the courtesans of capitalism' – the hedge funds.

After the tech bubble burst, the next 'fad' that hit financial markets was hedge funds – esoteric entities that have become so much the talk of the chattering classes, if not in Ireland then most certainly in other Western economies.

What are they? Hedge funds are simply investment vehicles that can deploy a much wider range of investment techniques in the pursuit of returns. The first hedge fund can be traced back to Alfred Winslow Jones, a journalist who first became interested in the stock market in the 1940s. In 1949 he founded A.W. Jones & Co. and began selling 'long and short'. What differentiated Jones's style of investing was his technique of

1.1. The Big Pieces

being 'long',* those stocks he liked, and 'short',† those he believed would fall in value – playing both sides if you will. His basic approach remains the most common of hedge funds today. Yet hedge funds remained on the sidelines for decades. Not until the late 1980s and early 1990s did the investing public become aware of hedge funds and awareness was limited to the actions of some of the very largest – notably George Soros's Quantum funds, held responsible for breaking the Bank of England's strong Sterling policy.

The notoriety gained by the more exuberant parts of the hedge fund world left the more mundane trading activities of most in the shade and left the public with a misconception, still shared today even by some professionals.

Despite its 'Gordon Gekko' caricature, from these relatively obscure beginnings, the capital markets spawned new methods of investing that are fast becoming mainstream. Amongst the exotic sounding types of hedge funds that now prowl in search of 'absolute returns' are long-short hedge funds, global-macro managers, convertible arbitrage, merger arbitrage, fixed income arbitrage, statistical arbitrage, short only, commodity trading advisors (CTAs) and market-neutral managers.

Yet their emergence was not a rapid one. In fact in 1984, there were believed to be no more than sixty-eight such funds in existence. Latest estimates put that number closer to 7500 (over 1500 greater than mutual funds).

I've devoted a particularly long section to hedge funds in Chapter 2 – in no small part as I believe that the techniques used will become increasingly 'mainstream' in years to come.

Private Equity

Most of us know of publicly quoted shares as 'equities', but there is another less well known part of the equity market that also plays a role for many investors – 'private equity'.

Private equity is quite simply unquoted equity – shares that exist only in private hands. As an industry, private equity investment is comparatively

---

* An investor is said to be long a stock when they have bought it and hold it to achieve gains from price increases.

† An investor shorts a stock by borrowing the security, selling it, and promising to return it at a point in the future, thereby standing to gain from a fall in price.

small, select and exclusive by comparison to the public markets. Yet despite its relatively small scale there are billion dollar funds out there run by names such as Blackstone, Carlyle, JP Morgan, Warburg Pincus, amongst others who specialise in one or both of the two forms of private equity investing.

This sector is comprised of two principal types of investment – buy-outs and venture. Buy-out firms, or leveraged buy-outs to give them their full title, are investors who spot a company that can do better. They purchase it or a part of it, often change or advise the existing management, usually introduce greater leverage, sometimes merge it with other firms and, using all these techniques, create investment value. (Firms involved in this sector are the ones made infamous, some would say unkindly, in the 1987 film *Wall Street*.) Venture firms are the first step on the road for new businesses and provide seed support and often management advice to start-up businesses.

Commodities

Whether one's concerned with grains, livestock, the much maligned pork bellies, coffee, juices, milk, cocoa or sugar, much of what finds its way onto our breakfast and dinner tables can also be invested in. A great deal of what goes into our cars and buildings also have their market place – metals, lumber, oils and gas. The measurements of exchange and price – currencies and financial indices – also form part of the huge tradable world that make up the futures markets.*

Any commodity I've mentioned can be invested in via the futures markets. The futures markets came about originally to help farmers, international traders and others to hedge their exposures. So if you were an orange grower in Florida, the futures market gave you a way to be a little more certain about the price you would get for your produce, whether your crop weathered a hurricane or not. Over time, these markets grew into vast trading arenas in which hedgers, traders and speculators could come together to provide pricing and insurance on commodities into the future.

---

* Futures contracts are agreements between two parties to commit to sell a commodity or security to the other at a given price and on a specified future date. Such contracts are traded in markets across the world.

1.1. The Big Pieces

The futures markets that emerged also saw the development of options* markets and eventually led to the complex web of derivative transactions that underpin much of today's financial system.

Introducing some Quasi-Science

When one looks at investment institutions from the outside, there is an expectation that someone in there 'knows the formula'. In most financial institutions the gentlemen with large foreheads do indeed spend a lot of time crunching numbers and sweating over whether Coca-Cola is earning $2.30 per share or $2.40 per share and should be priced at $40 or $50. And yes, there are many formulae, some of them very long and most of them impossible to remember. Unfortunately, like much scientific endeavour, once you've taken the time to learn and understand the formulae you then discover that they don't really work that well. In fact, in contrast to other fields where mathematics can be so massively influential, when it comes to managing personal wealth, while necessary, the math tends to be a somewhat blunt instrument. It helps to make some sense of things, but does not provide infallible answers. Nonetheless the tools and techniques used are powerful in the manner that they shape the way sensible investment is undertaken.

One of the most cited academics in this field is Harry Markowitz, whose pioneering work in developing optimisation techniques for balancing risk and reward still resonates today. Professor Markowitz published an article in the *Journal of Finance* in 1952 entitled 'Portfolio Selection'.[7] This work, which earned him the Nobel Memorial Prize in Economics, demonstrated that one of the most important features of investment decisions was not so much what an individual security was likely to do but how a portfolio of securities of all kinds could best be put together to optimise the return for the amount of risk that an investor would be prepared to take.

Prior convention for portfolio managers had been to gather together as many individually 'good deals' as possible for a client, without paying much regard to how these securities interacted. The 'modern portfolio theory' practice was to concentrate on how the basket of securities interacted together to produce risk and return. It's a lesson still lost on many professional and amateur investors alike.

---

* Options are contracts under which one party gives another party the right (but not the obligation) to buy or sell at a given price in the future.

Extrapolating the principles underlying 'Portfolio Selection' into financial planning is relatively simple:

- Assets tend to react to market circumstances in some related fashion (statisticians call it 'correlation') – in other words they move together to some extent.
- Assets tend to display a certain level of ups and downs (standard deviation).

Using these two measures, one can work out the minimum measurable risk for a given return, albeit crudely.

This sounds simple. However, while I'll spare you the maths, suffice to say it can only be accurate in the rear-view mirror. Unfortunately no one can be accurate about the inputs into such a calculation looking into the future. One can be informed by how things panned out in the past, particularly under certain sets of economic conditions, but certainty does not come with the kit.

Nonetheless few professional investors do not get exposure to the modern portfolio theory that developed in academic circles and the thinking is well ingrained in the psychology of financial planners.

What's more frustrating is that, while some of the framework that Professor Markowitz left to us is useful to address what individual business owners should do with their investment portfolios, we also know that human beings are not programmed in the manner that modern portfolio theory would like and there are plenty of limitations that mean we don't always do the most mathematically elegant thing. The work provided by the more recent 'behavioural finance' academics will help show some of the things you are likely to do whether rational or not!

Of course like all good science, once discovered and picked over by academics world-wide, the theories found their detractors – most agree that the principles are reasonably sound, but that to use such maths in an overly precise fashion is folly.

1.2. Putting Humpty Dumpty back together again

When you break out the various asset classes with all of their differing characteristics and you then ask, 'well, how do I get the best out of these?', you are asking a question that remains unsolved by finance academics,

1.2. Putting Humpty back together again

financial professionals and charlatans alike. Part I of the book – 'Making Sense of Capital Markets' – is devoted to helping you come up with some answers, however imperfect, to help you to build a solid, long-term wealth management strategy. This raises a number of questions. Firstly, what sort of return might be expected of each asset class? Secondly, how is each one likely to move in relation to the others? To get to these answers we'll need a bit of crystal ball gazing and a good deal of insight.

Having done all that we'll be in a position to put Humpty Dumpty back together again. At this stage we'll have to figure out where all the bits go and what they might do. The second section of the book – 'Putting Your Plans in Place' – deals with how you might glue the bits back together again, explaining many of the practical financial planning and tax issues with which business owners should have some familiarity.

NOTES

1. (2002) 3rd edition, UK: McGraw Hill.
2. (2002) Princeton, New Jersey: Princeton University Press.
3. (2005) 2nd edition, Princeton, New Jersey: Princeton University Press.
4. Benjamin Graham and David Dodd (1996), *Security Analysis* (the Classic 1934 Edition), US: McGraw-Hill.
5. Investopedia.com 'The Florida Real Estate Craze', <http://www.investopedia.com/features/crashes/crashes4.asp>, accessed 4/11/06.
6. International Monetary Fund (2003) 'When Bubbles Burst' (Chapter 2) *World Economic Outlook: Growth and Institutions*, April 2003, <http://www.imf.org/external/pubs/ft/weo/2003/01/pdf>, accessed 24/10/06.
7. Vol. 7, March 1952, pp 77–91.

CHAPTER 2

Resetting your Expectations from 2007 Onwards

2.1. From 2007 Onwards – Through the Looking Glass

Writing or advising about investments during the 1980s and 1990s produced a formula which proved correct time and again – in the long run equities go up. It has been followed by a second formula in the late 1990s and early 2000s – property always goes up.

Of course, equity markets would go through turbulent periods such as 1987, 1990, 1994, 1997, 1998 and would lose value for periods of time. Some of these periods lasted a couple of years but every time the bounce came it was a thing of beauty to behold. Equally the bond market would go through periods of losses, such as 1994 and 1998. However over the longer run, equities and to a lesser extent bonds would deliver positive returns and, when combined, they provided a relatively steady formula. Indeed it has proven a powerful formula for investors through perennial uncertainty. Many asset managers talk about the fact that the market almost always bails them out – and in so many respects this has proven true in recent decades. Equally property as an asset class has shown itself one directional for many years, leaving investors with a feeling of knowing much better than the professionals after a decade of appreciation in prices.

From the 1980s onwards, equities in particular began to get a lot of attention and a lot of added allocation from professional investors. Yes, periodically, headlines would appear on the Six O'Clock News featuring sweaty traders on the floors of the New York Stock Exchange and we'd then be treated to a crossover to Dublin's sleepy exchange for a local economist's viewpoint. This was great media, with newscasters peppering their discourse with verbs more befitting a theme park – 'plunging from heights to see dizzying losses mount throughout frenetic hours'. Mysterious red and green boxes twinkled on the screens of fresh-faced, red-braced yuppies.

But what all of this served to do was to disguise the much longer-term trend in the eyes of the investing public, a trend that began in the dark days of 1980–1981 when Ronald Reagan and Margaret Thatcher's economic thinking began the process of disinflation. It's difficult to remember what those days were like from the comfortable vantage point of the post-Celtic Tiger era: mass unemployment really starting to bite in Ireland; double digit interest rates; mass emigration; miners' strikes in England; the Troubles; hunger strikes; war in the Falklands; US industry on the scrapheap; Japan buying everything in sight. Disinflation began in the context of this uneasy environment. This longer-term trend was one that served the equity, bond and property markets well and was at the root of a two decade long surge in values. But it was not a trend that was obvious from the vantage point of 1981.

As monetarism tightened everyone's belts, inflation began to ease and with it we began to see the long-term decline of interest rates to normal levels as the inflationary excesses of the 1970s were truly extinguished. The trend of falling interest rates was of course far from a straight line event – in many periods during the past two decades we have seen rates ebb and flow. But there is no denying, with the benefit of hindsight, that we have seen a structural change in the nature of the world economy, perhaps returning to the low interest environment that prevailed quite literally for centuries before the inflation of the 1970s hit.

We may be stepping into a world that appears somewhat 'through the looking glass', as far as some of the shibboleths of modern financial advice are concerned.

2.2. The Building Blocks of Financial Asset Returns

Before hazarding a guess at what equities might do in the future, lets go back a couple of steps and try to understand what makes up financial asset returns. Richard Grinold of Barclays Global Investors suggests that there are five building blocks behind the returns of various financial assets.[1] I like to think of these in terms of the compensation you have to get because you are giving your money to someone else:

- The real rate of interest – the return that you'd get by lending your money to the Government.
- Inflation – the bit that the Government invisibly takes back by making money more readily available and hence less valuable.

2.2. The Building Blocks of Financial Asset Returns

Figure 2.1: Decomposing Expected Returns into Risk Premiums

Equity Market	Expected Equity Risk Premium
Corporate Bonds	Expected Credit Risk Premium
T-Notes	Expected Term Premium
T-Bills	Expected Inflation
Implied by TIPS	Expected Real Rate of Interest

Source: R.C. Grinold (2004), 'Closing the Gap between Expected and Possible Returns', *AIMR Conference Proceedings: Integrating Hedge Funds into a Private Wealth Strategy* (Feb 2004), Vol. 2004, No. 1, CFA Institute, pp. 33–42. Copyright © 2004, CFA Institute. Reproduced and republished from AIMR Conference Proceedings with permission from CFA Institute. All rights reserved.

- A term premium – because you have to get paid for giving your money away to the Government for a longer period.
- A credit risk premium – because you have to get paid for the possibility that you won't get your money back if you lend it to a company.
- The equity risk premium – because you have to get paid for a company losing this money as they don't have to give it back to you.

What's handy about most of the first four is that they are at least measurable and visible at a point in time in the market. You can see what they are right now and you can at least get a handle on them from the markets in terms of what expectations are. We can get the expected real rate of interest by looking out for the return on inflation protected bonds (TIPS – Treasury Inflation-Protected Securities) in the US and in Europe, a version of French OATs.* We can strip out what inflation is expected to be by simply deducting the yields on TIPS/OATs from Treasury bills. Compare that to longer-term bonds and then you have an estimate of what the term premium is, and then again to corporate bonds to get a sense of what the expected credit risk

---

* *Obligations Assimilables du Trésor* (OATs), a form of French government bond, a subset of which is issued as inflation-linked securities and is one of a number of inflation-linked bonds available in Europe including the UK, Greece, France, Italy and in 2005, Germany.

premium is. Of course there will be lots of variations in which bond to use and so on, but the broad brushstroke picture is a useful picture to carry with you.

One way of looking at this problem is to look back at history and assume that the past will repeat itself. Using the long-term yield on government bonds (5.7 per cent) and the historical equity risk premium (7.4 per cent) gives an expected future return of 12.1 per cent. Then subtract inflation of, say, 3 per cent and we get an expectation of stock market returns of about 9 per cent.

We could take that approach and you could go on to the second section of the book, which is a bit more factual. However, what such history fails to do is to recognise that, at least in financial terms, it is most unlikely to repeat itself in a very exact manner. The environment we look into now may have similarities to others, but it cannot be identical. There are changes afoot in the global economy that weren't at issue ten, twenty or thirty years ago. Just for starters, we did not have a Chinese economy on the brink of becoming a truly global economic power with the attendant inflationary and deflationary pressures. We did not have technology-led productivity on the scale now possible; we did not have a population of six billion to feed, nor did we have a rapidly ageing population. We did not have a single currency in Europe, nor a decline in the nation-state coupled with a commensurate rise in supranational sovereignty of large corporations. We did not have a single, unfettered superpower (at least not in the last 500 years), nor near unanimity on the most effective way to manage our economies. In Ireland, we did not have wealth on the scale now evident; we did not have an average income per head nearing the top of the European table or a quality of life at the top of the world tables (though they clearly haven't heard about our commuting times), nor did we have a burgeoning entrepreneurial class. We did not import capital from the US at the pace we now do, nor did we face the social challenges of immigration and a multi-cultural society. All of this makes the world a different place for the business owner who might be concerned about how to manage his or her wealth.

An investor at the start of the 1970s would have seen a very different place. He would have looked back at two decades of strong equity returns and muted inflation and might have concluded that he needed more stock market investments and property. Inflation ravaged that assumption and by the mid-1970s the business magazine *Business Week*[2] had headlined with the question 'Are Equities Dead?' after years of poor returns.

History may be instructive for us but it is not doomed to repeat itself when it comes to making informed choices for investment of your private wealth. Instead we need to find some ways of analysing what the current environment might mean for investors as well as learning from comparable environments in the past. Central to any intelligent discussion about what the long-term holds for investment are inflationary expectations, the interest rate environment and the equity risk premium. As a starting point the markets themselves give some very strong indications about what each of these might be in the near future.

2.3. Know your OATs

At time of writing the Euro-zone-wide expected inflation over the next decade, as indicated by the French inflation-linked OATs, runs at about 2 per cent and the expected real rate of interest at about the same over the same time frame.

By looking at the government yield curve in Europe, we can get a sense of what might be available from government bonds if you're prepared to go out over a slightly longer term. Take the five year bond and you'll probably find another 0.5 per cent. So far we've reached the lofty return of about 4.5 per cent. This is where it begins to get very tricky. The next step is into corporate bonds to determine how much more might be earned if we take on the risk of a company not paying its bills as opposed to a government so doing. To get a read on this we'll have to look into 'credit spreads': the gap in yield to maturity between government and corporate bonds of comparable term. Over the past few years, as the bond market figured that the chances of a company defaulting had actually risen as the global economy cooled, credit spreads had widened and indeed offered some terrific investment opportunities. More recently that reversed somewhat as the fortunes of the world economy took a turn for the better. In 2005 as the big US motor firms' debt was downgraded to junk status, the world's credit markets grew fidgety again and spreads began to widen once more. Matters subsequently calmed again and, at time of writing, credit spreads remain considerably narrower than historical norms. For simplicity let's take an average spread for a BBB-rated* company at about 0.75

---

* BBB is a 'credit rating'. Credit ratings are designed to provide investors with a measurement of the level of risk associated with a security or firm. An 'AAA' rating indicates a high level of security, a 'C' rating would indicate a much higher level of risk that the security might default on its obligations.

per cent. That adds up to just over 5 per cent that can be expected from a slightly risky corporate bond over the next few years, a real return of about 3 per cent.

While the actual figures will change periodically, what is important is the overall scale; by comparison to other periods, the quantum of return available from financial assets is now comparatively small. If one accepts that the disinflationary processes that have been in place for the past two decades have driven interest rates to a trough from which they will go no lower, then investors must look elsewhere for returns. Even a proportionately large increase in inflation or widening of credit spreads is unlikely to signal a prolonged period of gains from financial assets.

2.4. Equities – The Incredible Shrinking Equity Risk Premium

The French philosopher Alexis de Tocqueville once famously said '…une idée fausse, mais claire et precise, aura toujours plus de puissance dans le monde qu'une idée vraie mais complexe.'[3] This roughly translates as 'a false idea put across clearly and precisely is more powerful in the real world than a correct but complex one.' Put more pithily, people like sound bites and ideas that can be easily digested and even accepted as conventional wisdom, whether they make sense or not.

For financial planners the simple idea that has become mantra is: 'equities go up in the long run'. It has always been thus and thus shall it always be (though a more recent Irish version has suggested 'property always goes up in a straight line'!). It is a compellingly simple concept. Yes, equities will go up and down more in the short term but, if you stick with it, then things will improve in the long run and eventually markets will deliver stronger returns than you could have imagined. This has been proven massively correct for the best part of this century. And not just in the USA, where arguably the long-term returns had to be that bit better, given that it was a new continent a century ago and its industry was bound to generate new wealth. No, equities have proven just as good at generating better returns in almost every country where equity markets exist. Even after the bursting of the bubble from 2000–2002, this orthodoxy has remained well ensconced – ironically in no small part because aggregate levels of wealth were maintained by the soaring property market.

2.4. Equities – the Incredible Shrinking Equity Risk Premium

The most sought-after measure in the world of academic finance is the 'equity risk premium'. Whether this number will ever be accurately determined is a moot point. Understanding the measure and what it may mean for investors is essential to the toolkit of any financial advisor or business owner looking to gain insight into the future of their wealth. The simplest definition of the equity risk premium is that it is the reward that investors require to compensate the risk associated with holding equities compared to government securities – pretty straightforward really, or so you'd imagine. Alas, not so.

Stephen A. Ross wrote, 'What I actually think is that our prey, called the equity risk premium, is extremely elusive.'[4] In a needle-in-a-haystack-like search, academics around the world have become fascinated with how to evaluate what the equity risk premium will be in the future. If it can be effectively modelled the implications are enormous, as we can then hope to understand the likely return of equity markets, the likely return of bond markets and consequently plan efficiently for all our futures. This is a noble pursuit indeed. However, the most sought-after things are often the most elusive and there is no agreement at all as to what it actually is.

In most advanced markets we have reliable data stretching back between 100 and 200 years, depending on the country, all of which supports a persistent long-term equity risk premium somewhere in the region of 5–8 per cent. The other persistent phenomenon over the past century has been the fact that the equity premium that resulted was nearly always better than the return that had been expected. In short, investors were rewarded by a greater amount than they had expected or required by taking on the risk of the equity market. The 'equity risk premium puzzle' suggests that, in fact, equity investors have gotten persistently better rewards than the risks merited.

A quick tour around some of the views expressed by academics in this field will help. Professor Jeremy Siegel of the Wharton Business School (he of *Stocks for the Long Run* fame – see Chapter 1, Section 1.1) predicted in 2004 that the equity risk premium will shrink in the future because of low current dividend yields and high equity valuations, positing a real equity risk premium of circa 2–3% (circa 5% can be inferred assuming 2% inflation).[5] Also in 1999 Professor Cornell argued for a significantly lower risk premium of 4–5 per cent, up to 3 per cent below historical norms.[6] In 2002 Eugene F. Fama and Kenneth R. French also drew on a long period of time (1872–1999), and forecast an expected geometric equity risk premium of between 2.5 and 4.3 per cent.[7] Also in 2001, Robert D. Arnott and Ronald Ryan argued that the equity risk premium would actually turn negative based on low current dividend yields and low dividend growth in the future.[8] Wider survey results amongst finance academics yielded a slightly more optimistic risk premium of 4 per cent and one of the chief financial officers saw a range between 3.9 and 4.7 per cent.

What's most striking amongst all of these forecasts is the fact that all are a considerable distance behind the historical norms for the equity risk premium. Only a measure stretching back two centuries in scope provides a comparable level of premium using a long-term lens. Table 2.1 summarises the historic risk premium in the USA for a variety of long-run periods.

Only in the 1970s and early 1980s did we see comparable levels of premium actually realised over shorter periods (and by shorter I mean twenty year periods!).

What could cause equity returns to be so much more muted than in the past? In my view it is highly probable that equity returns will be lower for the next generation than they were in the past two decades. Not negative by any means, but less impressive. The following points, drawing on the

Table 2.1: Real U.S. Equity Markets and Riskless Security Returns and Equity Risk Premium, 1802–2000

Period	Mean Real Return on Market Index	Mean Real Return on Relatively Riskless Asset	Risk Premium
1802–1998	7.0%	2.9%	4.1%
1889–2000	7.9	1.0	6.9
1889–1978	7.0[a]	0.8	6.2[b]
1926–2000	8.7	0.7	8.0
1947–2000	8.4	0.6	7.8

[a]Not rounded, 6.98 per cent.
[b]Not rounded, 6.18 per cent.
Source: Rajnish Mehra (2001), *The Equity Risk Premium Forum Conference Proceedings* (November 2001), AIMR (now CFA Institute), pp. 60–66. Copyright © 2001, CFA Institute. Reproduced and republished from The Equity Risk Premium Forum with permission from CFA Institute. All rights reserved.

2.4. Equities – the Incredible Shrinking Equity Risk Premium

contributions of many commentators, offer explanations as to why this will be the case.

The Post-2000 Equity Market is the Early Part of a Secular Bear Market

The deflation of the equity bubble in the late 1990s was inevitable and probably welcome in the sense that if it had continued it would have had even more lasting and damaging effects on the world economy. As it stands we still face considerable problems of pension funding deficits and lost life savings.

Figure 2.2 shows P/E for the US since 1871. Arnott makes some adjustments to the graph to help make things more directly comparable between low inflation and high inflation periods. Whatever way you look at this chart, the story about the late 1990s doesn't get any prettier and the

Figure 2.2: P/E Based on Smoothed 10-year Real Earnings, 1971–September 2006

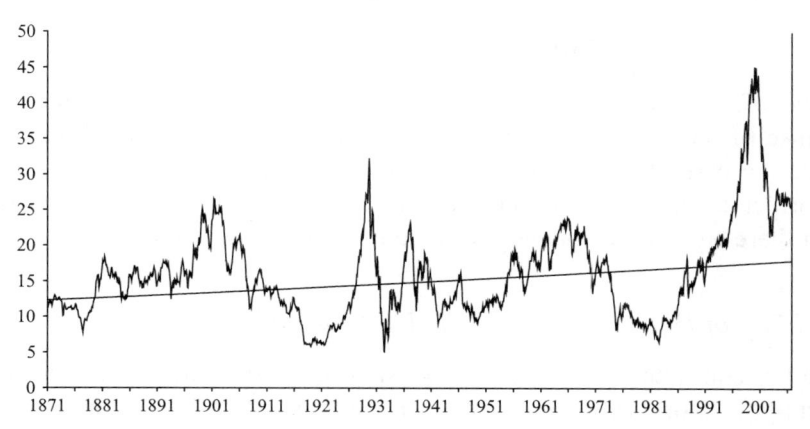

Source: Robert D. Arnott (2004), 'Managing Assets in a World of Higher Volatility and Lower Returns', *CFA Conference Proceedings: Points of Inflection – New Directions for Portfolio Management* (July 2004), Vol. 2004, No. 4, pp. 39–52. Copyright © 2004, CFA Institute. Reproduced and republished from Points of Inflection: New Directions for Portfolio Management with the permission of CFA Institute. All rights reserved. Updated version with data to Q3 2006 provided courtesy of Robert Arnott.

current picture remains on the wrong side of the average for an overly bullish position. It was extraordinary by any historical standards. What's also worth noting, as Arnott does in his analysis, is that a chart such as this shows us two things. Firstly, it displays a great deal of short-term bull and bear markets, with bull markets dominating and typically lasting three to five years, followed by bear markets typically of a slightly shorter duration and frequency. Secondly, it shows us the secular bull and bear markets, the much longer-term trends that are apparent in markets with secular bull markets lasting 20–30 years. Arnott and Ryan point to 'secular peaks' having occurred in 1901, in 1929 and again in 1965. They also point out that secular bear markets have historically lasted '17–20 years...spanning three to five bull and bear market cycles....' They suggest that secular bear markets don't really finish until valuations in markets get cheap, a level that even the most ardent bulls admit was never reached in the rout of 2000–2002.[9] Hence, optimists have reason to be more constrained and we may find the equity market can only grind out modest returns from present levels, at least in the aggregate. (That's not to say that investors won't periodically make strong returns from equities, but it won't be as easy.)

Inflation is on the way back

Some of the most respected views in the bond market predicted the demise of the secular disinflationary trend that was in place effectively since the early 1980s. While it would be over-dramatic, indeed wholly incorrect, to suggest a return of high inflation, there is good cause to suggest there are pivotal changes en route in the coming years.

Build up of Debt has Fuelled the US Consumer

The US consumer was largely responsible for lifting the US and consequently the world economy away from the threat of deflation that loomed in 2002. Figure 2.3 shows the extent of the growth in household debt in the US. The spending spree, which came courtesy of much private debt that has since acted as a spur to corporate earnings, was financed in no small part by overseas investors' insatiable appetite for American securities. Witness the level of ownership of US treasuries by foreigners, mostly from Asia (that of itself should not be a concern – some would say it is soothing to know that non-Americans now have to lie awake worrying

2.4. Equities – the Incredible Shrinking Equity Risk Premium

Figure 2.3: U.S. Household Sector Debt as a Percentage of Personal Disposable Income

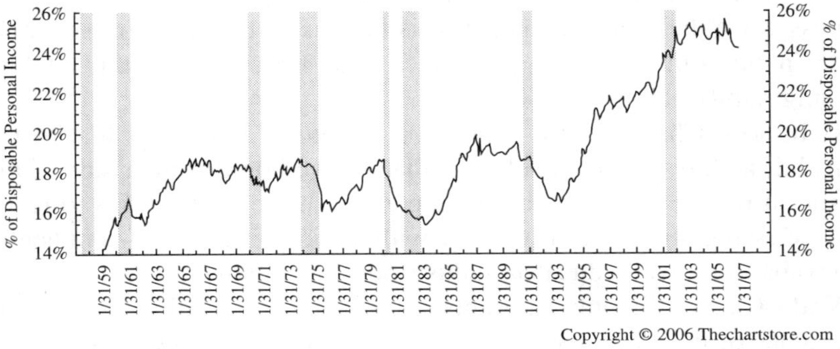

Source: <http://www.thechartstore.com>

about the US economy; that they are in emerging markets might be cause for thought).

Excess Liquidity

The global economy came close to deflation during 2002 and was bailed out by the US printing presses' roll out of hundred dollar bills in the form of 1 per cent Fed Funds and relaxation of US fiscal policy into a $500 billion+ deficit. The consequential weakening of the dollar was dramatic and only by mid-2005 did this decline relent. At time of writing dollar uncertainty was again making headlines and it could remain a theme for some time for markets. In the very long run, a nation that chooses to be a debtor in this fashion will most likely see its currency fall in relative value.

All of this is being financed from somewhere and much of the source of the imbalance emanates from the Far East, as a result of the emergence of China and its knock-on stimulatory impact on its neighbours, most importantly the previously moribund Japanese economy. Nobody rationally doubts that China's emergence will fail to reshape global economics – only political mismanagement will halt the trend that has begun. If it reaches South Korea's level of development in a half century it will still be four times bigger than the US economy. However over-investment, volatility and overheating will all feature on its path to becoming a developed economy (as is always the case), assuming that it does continue on that path. Even now, China is more highly leveraged than the US economy – 200 per cent debt to GDP by crude estimates – and that leverage is most prominently expressed via the property market. It is that, as well as the unsustainable surge in investment, which presents a risk, with its potential bubble-popping ramifications.

Right now, China, with a population of four to five times that of the USA, has a GDP just one twelfth of that enjoyed on the other side of the Pacific. It only has to grow by three per cent more than the US to reach half the living standards in the US within forty-five years – eminently achievable for a well-educated, industrious population.

While China still only accounts for 4 per cent of global GDP, the emergence of its consumer society is creating unprecedented demand for commodities – 20–30 per cent of the world's cement; nearly as much steel, coal and iron ore; and 7 per cent of all the oil. (This is reason alone for investors to consider commodities in their portfolio, although this will not be a one-way bet in the short term.) Indeed Japan's re-emergence from deflationary recession is in many respects borne out of its neighbour's fledgling wealth with some estimates suggesting that 40–50 per cent of Japanese growth is China-centric.

The argument for long-term growth globally hinges somewhat on China/Asia picking up the baton from the ageing, increasingly debt-fattened and soon-to-be equity-consuming Europe and US. But for Asia to have a meaningful impact they, along with India, will have to get used to consuming as opposed to saving (historically their preference). And China is not without its own demographic difficulties: it will be amongst the most rapidly ageing populations in the world within a decade, a fact exacerbated by the official retirement age for common labourers of fifty-five for men and fifty for women.

Whatever way one looks at this, a slowdown from the US consumer is a possibility, perhaps a probability. Either further dollar devaluation or a pullback in the purchase of US Treasuries could be precipitating factors since higher interest rates necessarily eat into consumer purchasing power. Both could be caused by a cooling in the Far East.

What is probably fair to say, however, is that the deficits the US Government has chosen to produce for the past five years are more profligate than that country can perhaps wisely maintain. It presents an

2.4. Equities – the Incredible Shrinking Equity Risk Premium

imbalance in the global economy that appears unlikely to be sustainable in the very long run. That the medicine the US might need is either an adjustment in the dollar to weaker levels or higher taxes presents really only one choice and the adjustment is more likely to be via the exchange rate. If that occurs it may once again protect the US economy – but it may prove less supportive of US denominated investment by foreigners.

Doomsayers would have one believe that a dollar collapse will be the consequence of the emerging markets in the East. Lest all this sound Cassandra-like, it is probably useful to remember the timescales over which the rebalancing of the global economy will take place. Henry Kissinger was once heard to have asked Chairman Mao whether he thought the French Revolution had been a success. Mao's legendary reply was: 'It's too early to tell'. Perhaps that is the type of timescale the Chinese have in mind when it comes to the dollar.

It is not in the interest of any of the emerging economies to see the US economy or the Dollar weakened dramatically in a short period of time – such an outcome would be catastrophic to their development. Instead the self interest of these economies will be served by a slow and very gradual rebalancing of the dollar as the productive capabilities of these markets develop.

Add this up and the case for instability can be argued as arising from:

- continued US consumer leverage dependent on cheap financing;
- continued US securities held overseas;
- weak dollar, strong euro (or least instability until the Eastern currencies revalue and allow the imbalances to right themselves);
- European unwillingness to free markets and reduce scale of social welfare states;
- continuance of below potential Continental European economic growth;
- more geopolitical instability;
- more risk of a slowdown/shock in Asia.

Under this scenario, on balance, we'll see greater inflation (albeit modest), perhaps greater state involvement in the US, greater liberalisation in Europe (albeit modest) and modest interest rate increases on both sides of the Atlantic (although in the shorter run, the process of tightening may be coming to a close in the US and may be quite short-lived in Europe). It is important not to confuse short-term cyclicality with longer, secular trends and I believe we are seeing that change coming about.

We've seen as much as a 3 per cent adjustment in the US in recent times. If we see further substantive rate increases (greater than two per cent globally) in the coming couple of years (quite low probability) the adjustment could involve a reduction in capital values in most markets. Any higher and the already narrowed/negative yield gap between commercial property yields and cost of borrowing will tighten to a point where leveraged investors find the property market a less hospitable place. The US will almost certainly be impacted in this fashion, and the UK is arguably already in this position. Thankfully, the Eurozone is probably the most insulated with its sluggish growth rates acting as a bulwark against inflation and arguably Ireland's 'economic moat' may continue until a lack of competitiveness acts to constrain the growth here. Lack of competitiveness will emerge as local salaries continue to rise and local pockets are impacted by euro-led interest rates.

Sooner or Later Earnings will Revert, that's just Gravity

Corporate earnings growth rates of close to 30 per cent year-on-year are unsustainable when compared to long-term averages closer to 7 per cent. That's what I wrote in the first draft of this section at the end of 2004 and growth rates have indeed reduced to more normalised levels (circa 16 per cent was being cited in mid 2006). However just when rising oil prices and the threat of higher interest rates would suggest equities should be taking a beating, along come stronger earning numbers than expected. This underpinned stronger gains in 2005 and again in 2006 for investors. When you look at US corporate profitability (in current dollars adjusted for inventories and capital expenditures), the underlying trend points to the 2004–2005 earnings growth being high by historical standards and the rate beginning to normalise. By early 2006, though robust, earnings growth had reached less stratospheric levels. The market roared ahead again in early 2006, albeit in a narrow corridor focused primarily at the riskier end of the market, and finally broke down in May–June of 2006 with a significant retrenchment in these parts of the market. In the latter part of 2006 markets had returned to strong growth.

2.4. Equities – the Incredible Shrinking Equity Risk Premium

One can make the case that at current levels of valuation equity markets look comparatively cheap by the standards of recent history – certainly when compared to the past decade. However they may be cheap because earnings are about to turn down. As we can see from Figure 2.4, we've been through a number of years of very strong earnings growth and if history repeats itself we are due to see this slowing.

Nonetheless, corporate profitability is at the fourth highest level in current dollars since the 1970s. Previous highs have tended to revert over about two years, usually to below average levels. There's nothing to say that a very vibrant US economy cannot go from strength to strength but this conflicts with the records of previous good performances.

To argue for continued high earnings growth over a prolonged period one must also argue for a dramatic retrenchment in the role of government. This argument is perhaps better supported in the long run than in the immediate term.

Figure 2.4: The Profits Revival – Year-on-year Growth in After-Tax Profits

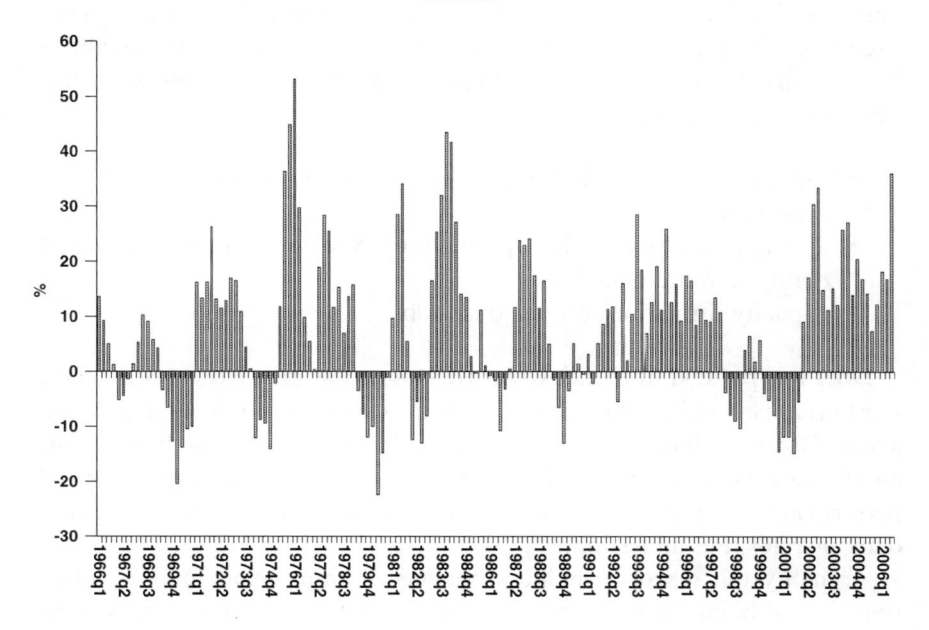

Source: Datastream.

Western Assets – Particularly Equities – are Overbought

The equity market movements of the 1990s were unprecedented as was the length of the bull market from 1982–2000. Bonds and property have also seen spectacular returns resulting from a secular shift from 1970s inflation to 1980s–2000 disinflation. Disinflation appears to have stopped sometime in the past two to three years.

During the past twenty years, all three major assets have risen as a consequence of:

- the long-term decline of inflation and interest rates after the unprecedented inflation of the 1970s;
- baby boom demographics in most Western economies;
- a rise in personal debt;
- a rise in productivity (although this is exaggerated compared to historical norms).

This was supported by the rise of mutual funds, the Internet, analyst optimism and accounting malpractice. The resulting bubble has since deflated. The consequence was a halving of valuations. This is good news except for the fact that even this colossal adjustment has only brought us back to just below the previous high (ahem, 1929). In contrast to this period we now face into:

- modest rise in global inflation fuelled by emergence of new economies;
- ageing populations in Europe and the US releasing large amounts of equity in retirement;
- capacity limitations on personal debt.

Does this portend further downturns? Not necessarily. However even the most optimistic writers have reined in their expectations of market performances. Optimists look to real returns of 5–7% before charges from public equity markets. At current levels of valuation it would take an unprecedented performance to get beyond this level of returns, as Figure 2.5 clearly demonstrates. Pessimists point lower.

Arguably the disconnectedness between earnings and market valuations is still being brought into line with longer-term norms and, as such, the risks of further downturns cannot be discounted. In short, the potential

2.4. Equities – the Incredible Shrinking Equity Risk Premium

Figure 2.5: Price Earnings Ratio Predicting Subsequent Ten-Year Real Returns Annual January Data, 1881–1990 (1891–2000 returns)

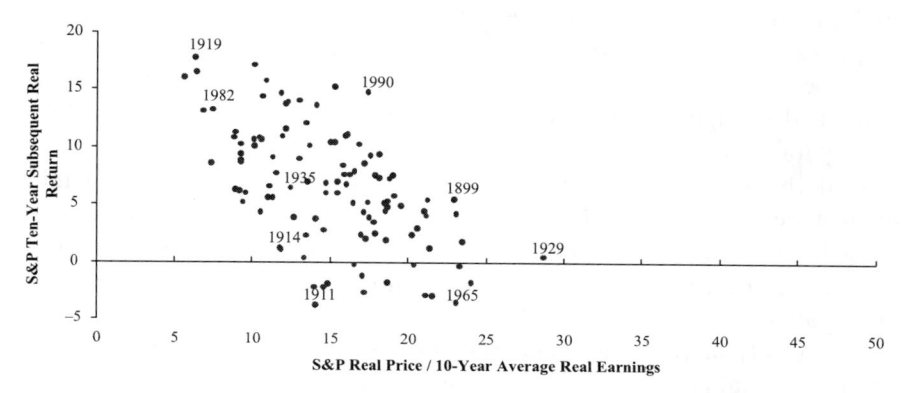

Source: From Campbell-Shiller presentation before Federal Reserve Board, 3 December 1996.

return that can be achieved from Western public equity markets (in the aggregate) relative to historic norms will be lower. At the very least, we must question whether Western public equities should remain as the predominant source of return for a business owner's investment portfolio, that is if one thinks 'in a straight line'. An environment where market indices drift has been seen many times before and many investors made their fortune through actively trading their portfolio. Such an environment prevailed from the mid 1950s until the 1980s but investors then made fortunes from more generous dividend policies and from buying and selling at the right time.

European markets do not paint quite as stark a difficulty but even here valuations are at roughly historic norms. What all that suggests is that there's not much juice left in the equity market in the aggregate, although there'll be plenty to be had in individual deals.

But then again, on the other hand ...

Before you run out and suggest to your stockbroker that he is a raving nutter and its time to sell, sell, sell, there is another school of thought that argues just as plausibly that the equity risk premium 'bears' have it all wrong.

In 2005, critics suggested that the circa seventeen times earnings multiples in markets were only sustained by extraordinary earnings growth/surprises and that, had earnings not surprised, then we would have seen up to 20 per cent downside. In 2006, despite less challenging valuations and continued strength in corporate earnings, markets rediscovered volatility and by mid-year had sold off all gains.

Underlying what has been happening in markets is a belief that the environment we are heading into is one in which corporate earnings growth will revert to its long-term mean of circa 7 per cent per annum. That would be bad news for the equity market if it happened faster than anticipated.

Conversely there are commentators that maintain that earnings growth from high quality companies is currently priced more generously than it has been for some time.

First published in 1962, Ben Graham's classic book *Security Analysis: Principles and Techniques* is instructive, particularly as he wrote it in an interest rate environment comparable to today's.

If Graham's appropriate P/E ratios are correct (see Table 2.2), we can see earnings growth slip back to 7 per cent from its most recent 27 per cent without multiple contraction of much note. If earnings growth is sustained even at a more modest pace then expansion is more likely.

Table 2.2: Graham's Table of Appropriate P/E Ratios

Expected rate of growth (for 7 years)	Multiplier of average (4th year) earnings	Multiplier of current earnings
3.5%	13x	15x
5.0%	14x	17x
7.2%	15x	20x
10.0%	16x	23.5x
12.0%	17x	27x
14.3%	18x	31x
17.0%	19x	35.5x
20.0%	20x	41.5x

Source: Benjamin Graham and David Dodd (1996), *Security Analysis* (the Classic 1934 edition), US: McGraw-Hill.

2.4. Equities – the Incredible Shrinking Equity Risk Premium

The Market is Overdoing it on Inflation

In the past couple of years interest rates have been at uncommonly accommodative levels. Nonetheless, we have seen considerable changes as the central banks oscillate between concerns for deflation and managing inflation.

By the end of 2004, bond yields (at least in the US and UK) were up over 1.5% since their low in summer 2003, when all the talk was of deflation. The central banks had all changed tone with the Fed continuing to indicate interest rate increases, the Bank of England suggesting there were more increases to come and the ECB indicating that it was unlikely to cut rates.

By mid-2005, as yields fell in Europe and the UK and the Fed did indeed continue to raise rates, the argument was once again to be heard that the inflation bogeyman had been contained (and held in the same control as his nastier deflationary cousin). At the end of 2005, yields were back up somewhat as the expectations for resurgent though modest inflation increased.

However, there is also a body of opinion that contends that the market is overdoing the threat of inflation.[10]

The market expectations for inflation in the US are mapped out clearly by the difference between inflation-linked bonds and comparable government bonds. This gap reached a low in summer 2003 at 1.4 per cent and increased to about 2.7 per cent in 2006 (the highest it has been since 1997).

Another argument touted in the media is that the depreciation of the dollar should spark imported inflation. The evidence does not support this thesis. In a paper delivered in May 2004 for the Shadow OMC,* evidence was presented that showed periods of dollar depreciation having no appreciable direct impact on US inflation.

Capacity Utilisation Suggests there's Plenty of Room before we see Inflation Soar

Until recently, by historical standards, US capacity utilisation (how much those folks in the US actually make compared to what they could make at full tilt) had been at a level last seen in the early 1980s and before that in

---

* The Shadow OMC (Open Market Committee) was founded by Prof. Karl Brunner of the University of Rochester and Prof. Allan Meltzer of Carnegie-Mellon University. It held its first semi-annual meeting on 14 September 1973. The original objective was to evaluate the policy choices and actions of the Federal Reserve's Open Market Committee (FOMC).

Figure 2.6: Capacity Utilisation in the US – Room to Grow?

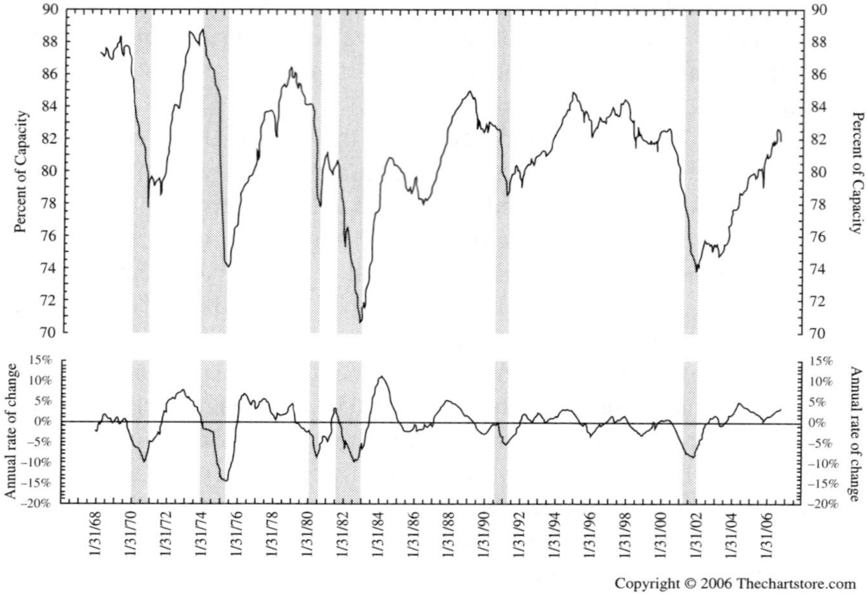

Source: <http://www.thechartstore.com>

the mid-1970s. However it has been playing catch-up for the last couple of years. Looking back two years, the spare capacity suggested the US economy could increase output significantly without supply issues arising that could add to inflation. So in theory they could increase output, work harder and prices could still stay pretty much the same. That's a very powerful argument. Underpinning it is the argument that all of the technological advances we have made in recent decades mean that we can expect a lot more money to run around our economies without creating the inflation that is so damaging. However the catch up in capacity utilisation suggested by the above charts might lead one to conclude that there's little room for error.

There have been plenty of periods of time when productivity gains have arisen, some more so than in recent years, but on few occasions has the world had the ability to make and do so much more without sparking inflationary pressures.

2.4. Equities – the Incredible Shrinking Equity Risk Premium

Figure 2.7: The FTSE 100 P/E 1996–2006

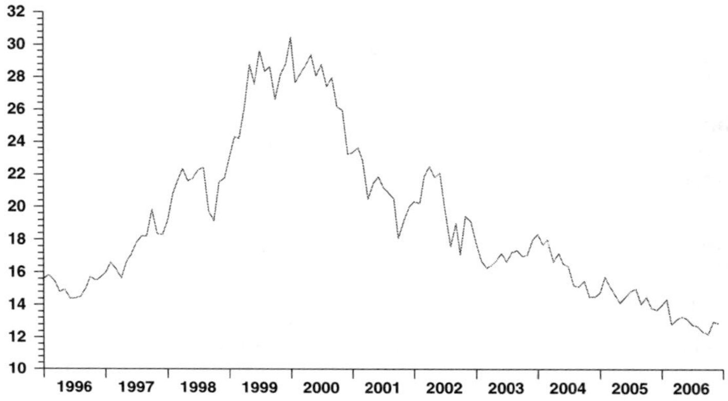

Source: Thomson Datastream.

The Bubble in Valuations is a Long Way Behind

When compared to recent history, equity markets today are vastly less expensive than the days when valuations were self-evidently in bubble territory. Take the UK for example, where multiples halved before rebounding.

With major markets at twelve to fourteen times prospective earnings in 2007 and looking into 2008, even if analysts are being a bit generous and even if they've omitted to include the pension deficit and option expenses in their calculations, things don't look overly stretched at all. In fact, at these levels, the equity market may present a better point of entry than has been seen for more than a decade, a point which will support a 'grinding out' of mid to high single digit returns from public equities.

Tightening doesn't mean the Market goes South

When rates are increased by central banks, economists talk of tightening of monetary policy. One doesn't have to look far beyond the next notch in the belt for an explanation of the phrase. The beginning of the end of the tightening cycle will be one of the keys to 2007–2008 equity, bond and property market prospects. The amount of inflation and the extent of the tightening will be key determinants in how your equity and property portfolios perform.

Table 2.3: Market Behaviour Six Months after the Fed's First Upward Move

	1997	1984	1986	1994	1999
Fed Funds bp	0.88	1.94	0.75	1.00	0.50
European rate bp	n/a	0.00	−0.50	−1.15	0.50
10 year US bond yield bp	n/a	0.82	1.57	1.36	0.58
10 year German bond yield bp	n/a	−0.11	−0.25	0.95	0.77
USD/DEM %	−7.9	10.6	−8.7	−8.9	2.7
GBP/DEM %	3.2	−1.9	3.7	−5.8	5.3
S&P 500 %	−9.9	5.3	16.6	−2.7	6.6
Datastream Europe %	14.3	−6.9	23.9	−2	17.5

Source: 'The Inflationary Threat' (2004), BNP Paribas.

At time of writing, the Fed appeared to have finished its measured moves (which it has been doing in predictable lot sizes of 0.25 per cent each time over recent years). There's even some (modest) possibility of things starting to head the other direction as the US economy slows in 2007. The market still thinks that the ECB will follow suit with perhaps 0.5% in increases into 2007. The cause of tightening is simple – economic indicators have beaten expectations worldwide, and across the US, Euroarea and UK, the medicine of historically abnormal liquidity pumped into the system since 2000 has finally delivered and kept the deflation bogeyman at bay. The doom-mongers maintain that this will cause already over-valued markets to react negatively. History is not on their side if one analyses the reaction of markets to periods of interest rate tightening over the past three decades. What's more, Europe is reacting to this medicine in an anaemic fashion and we may yet see stalling on the part of the ECB, although they will continue to harp on about their heightened state of vigilance.

In a paper published in May 2004, BNP reviewed the impact of tightening on financial markets in 1977, 1984, 1986, 1994 and 1999.[11] What is immediately apparent from Table 2.3 is the lack of uniformity in reaction from equity markets. US stocks rose in 1999, 1986 and 1984, but fell in 1994 and 1977; the dollar gained against the German Deutschemark in 1984, was relatively stable in 1999, and weakened in 1994, 1986 and 1977. This is not quite the mathematical relationship one might assume – it is simply untrue to argue that interest rate increases axiomatically mean trouble for equities.

2.4. Equities – the Incredible Shrinking Equity Risk Premium

Stocks might just be less risky than they used to be

Back in 1998, finance commentators struggled to legitimise the values that had been reached by the stock market. On 30 March 1998, the *Wall Street Journal* published an article by J.K. Glassman and K.A. Hassett arguing that the reason that the market had reached such heights was that the equity risk premium had actually fallen permanently and that, as a consequence, the market had to be at a higher level (their infamous expectation of 'Dow 36,000').

In his excellent book *The Equity Risk Premium*, published in 1999, Bradford Cornell explains the Glassman and Hassett argument well using a simple example. They assume that the risk-free rate of interest is 5 per cent to begin with, and that the equity risk premium is 8 per cent (the historical average in the US). They then assume that dividends are expected to grow by 5 per cent, made up of 3 per cent to compensate for inflation and 2 per cent real growth. Using these assumptions, they show that a drop of just 2 per cent in the risk premium (i.e. investors requiring just 6 per cent over the risk-free rate of interest for holding equities) would result in a 167 per cent increase in stock prices.

The argument goes on to maintain that, because the stock market has become highly regulated and highly liquid with perfectly transparent pricing, it has indeed become less risky than the market that existed in the 1920s.

Then along came the technology bubble crash and the scandals at Enron and Andersen, all of which left the equity risk premium seeming alive and well.

The expected risk premium is clearly elusive because of its ever-changing nature. It may have dropped temporarily in the 'flat-earth' thinking of the late 1990s but it came back with a vengeance once the accounting shenanigans undermined trust in the market. Add in 50 per cent losses and by 2003 the forward looking premium was once again to be seen. From the vantage point of 2006, three years into the equity bull run, the risk premium had rewarded investors once again. From the starting point of 2007, arguably risk premia have once again begun to fall back.

Earnings Yields Point to a Buy Signal for Equities

The bond/equity yield ratio compares the inverse of the P/E ratio to the thirty-year Treasury Bond yield. At present this ratio is close to 150 per cent,

Figure 2.8: The Bond-Equity Yield Ratio 1998–2006

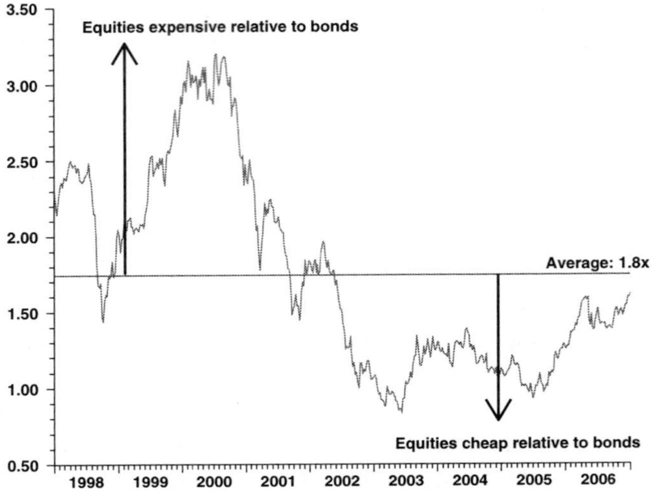

Source: Thomson Datastream 2006.

compared to a historical average closer to 180 percent. This measure has reached lows at periods of extreme over-valuation such as occurred in late 1999 and early 2000 and through mid-1987. While this measure has it detractors, at minimum it gives comfort that there isn't a sharp correction ahead. If this indicator is wrong it means that: a) bond markets haven't priced in sufficient interest rate increases in the long end of the curve; b) we are seeing a reversion to pre-1950s style equity yields (ie. above bond yields); c) earnings yields will dramatically reverse; or parts of all the above.

Figure 2.8 describes the bond/equity yield ratio comparing global bonds and global equities. On average since 1998 bonds yielded 1.8 times equities – what the graph shows is that equities relative to bonds look cheap by the standards of recent history.

Some Take-Away Advice

So, what is one to make of this? I'd suggest that there are perhaps five points that every business owner needs to take out of the last few pages.

2.4. Equities – the Incredible Shrinking Equity Risk Premium

i. Inflation is quite likely to make a comeback, but in midget form as it will be a far more benign and less threatening version than seen in the 1970s. Now retired, Alan Greenspan had been saying over the past few years that inflation is inevitable. Interest rates increases will follow and will find their way back to more normal non-hyper-stimulatory levels.
ii. Financial assets tend to 'like' falling interest rates; tangible assets tend to prefer inflationary environments. Hence bonds could face into a stronger headwind than has been seen for some time (although property and commodities may also have seen the best of the gains already). Equities won't do double digits that often, but are arguably the least over-valued from their mid-late 2006 starting point.
iii. Equities and bonds face a headwind of rising inflation and modestly higher interest rates, so you may want to adjust your sights when it comes to how well equities might perform. But don't give up on your shares yet; they remain an absolutely essential part of your portfolio and are the least expensive of the major asset classes at this juncture. They are also probably the only remaining part of your portfolio that could throw in occasional (strongly positive) surprises. Just don't believe anyone who says 10 per cent+per annum is possible year-in-year-out from the broad market. The broad market will struggle to generate this level; although there is a case for individual stock-picking that could significantly outperform.
iv. Alternative investing – hedge funds, private equity and commodities are all likely to become more mainstream and will be a welcome addition to the toolkit for all financial advisors; their principal use is to add diversity and new sources of return, but don't overdo it! Some alternative strategies have come a bit undone in the past year or two and their much-vaunted alchemic capabilities appear to be naked emperors.
v. Row back on any expectations you have of persistent double digit returns. They will not happen with any great frequency from here on without using dramatic levels of leverage or taking much greater market risk.

2.5. Property – The World's Greatest Asset or Smoke and Mirrors?

With its direct impact on everyone's fortunes and the emotional attachment that we, as a nation, have to property, it almost feels impolite to comment on its future in anything but glowing terms. Indeed in an Irish context one feels somewhat further handicapped by the fact that every bar stool and kitchen table has probably heard more opinions on this matter than I or anyone else in the wealth management industry has. That said, no book on wealth management would be complete without taking a tour into the property world, even if it does mean suggesting some downsides that not everyone will find palatable.

Firstly, however, it is necessary to take a detour into some of the economic history surrounding property markets. I will concentrate on facets of the UK, US, Japanese and Irish markets over the past three decades or so, taking a different perspective on each. Like all histories I believe this can help paint a backdrop to why the property market is as it is. That done, and as 'it's all about location' in the property market, some of the hot-spots around the world will be considered. I'll finish off by endeavouring to put property into a portfolio context.

A Potted Economic History of Major Property Markets

The UK Commercial Property Market since the War

In the UK after the war, as with many parts of Continental Europe, a building boom followed the devastation wrought across the major cities. Roughly three-quarters of a million square metres of office space had been destroyed in the aerial bombardment of Britain, leaving the country with an acute shortage after the war. By the 1950s, with interest rates low and commercial property scarce, the 'yield gap' (the difference between rents and the cost of finance) was substantial, attracting investment into the market. Short-term financing came from developers and from banks and longer-term fixed rate mortgage-based financing came from insurance companies. At this time much of the financing was entirely debt based. It was then that companies such as Land Securities (now a FTSE 100* company) became established

---

* FTSE 100 refers to the top 100 listed companies on the London Stock Exchange

2.5. Property – The World's Greatest Asset or Smoke and Mirrors?

and indeed some property companies were listed in the stock market, providing another source of capital. By the 1960s, as inflation began to rise, financial institutions began to take equity stakes in development companies, either by way of conversion rights or through joint venture companies. Sale and leaseback became a dominant arrangement as developers offered to sell the proposed building subject to the investor leasing it back. The office development boom was eventually contained, for political reasons, by the introduction of government controls by the then Labour Government in the mid-1960s.

In the run up to the stock market crash of 1974, new forms of property investment such as property unit trusts and bonds came available. Shortage of investment properties pushed all property related entities skywards and stimulated mergers in the sector. Also during that period, as inflation took hold, the nature of the standard property lease also changed, initially to fourteen years and then to seven and finally to five year reviews.

After the crash of 1974, the economic landscape changed fundamentally for property investors. Where low (albeit rising) inflation had supported long-term twenty to thirty year low interest rate mortgages, an environment of high inflation with commensurately high interest rates created a wildly different situation. Highly geared property companies, built for a different environment, did not withstand the increased capital costs and income voids that happened in the economic downturn. Both the direct property market and property related shares collapsed. For investors it was happening at the same time as an even more dramatic fall in the stock market and, with inflation in double digits, there was quite literally nowhere to hide. However by the late 1970s the market was on the rise again and the latter part of the decade saw an investment boom with large institutions, particularly insurance companies, active as developers.

In the 1980s and 1990s 'forward funding' became the usual approach to financing property development in the UK. Under this arrangement, the provider of the funds would purchase the site and provide a loan to finance the building. Interest would be rolled up during the development (at a 'keep' rate or a long-term interest rate) and on the completion and letting of the building the profit would be paid by the funder to the developer.

Another novel approach was the use of commercial indemnity insurance to increase the loan to value achievable; under such arrangements an insurer effectively takes on the risk of the extra part of the debt.

Despite these ways of reducing risk for property development and increasing lending, the UK continued in its boom/bust patterns and the early 1980s was not a good time for commercial property in the UK, with rental increases falling and yields rising. Despite 'green shoots of economic recovery' property lagged behind the rest of the economy. In particular the institutional investors had lightened their holdings of property significantly during this period – perhaps wisely given the boom that was occurring in the stock market. In fact, from an allocation of some 20 per cent in property in insurance company portfolios in 1980, the allocation had fallen back to just 7 per cent by the mid-1980s (and remained there or below ever since). This phenomenon repeated itself across most developed economies as institutions lightened their exposure to property as an asset class. In one survey covering ten developed economies the average allocation had halved from 8 per cent to 4 per cent between 1988 and 1996, with only France seeing an increase in allocation.[12] In the place of the investment institutions came the lending institutions. With significant liquidity available to them the banks lent to developers and allowed them roll up interest until the property was sold, a practice sometimes seen as the smoking gun behind the speculative activity that came into the market by the late 1980s and early 1990s. In the early 1990s vacancy rates soared and rents spiralled as the boom once again turned to bust. From 1990 to 1994 some fifteen of the quoted property companies in the UK went into insolvency with losses in values as high as 50 per cent in the London office market. Banks left the property market and property prices in the UK commercial sector again headed south, despite some efforts to provide greater liquidity to the market (including the introduction of property unit trusts and even futures contracts).

In September 1992, the pound was devalued and withdrew from the exchange rate mechanism, which prompted a recovery in the yield gap between the yields on commercial property and interest rates. This prompted speculation that there was another property rise on the cards and lifted interest amongst institutional and international investors.

By the late 1990s and early 2000s, the UK market was once again performing well as a falling interest rate environment and strong overseas private investor interest showed itself in volume. In particular, this interest was from the Middle East, Germany and Ireland, who between them account for about two thirds of the overseas investment.

2.5. Property – The World's Greatest Asset or Smoke and Mirrors?

The UK from 2007...

UK Commercial

Flows into the UK market have been strong and a combination of the weight of capital and the Bank of England reducing interest rates led to yield compression in the UK Commercial property market. Returns for investors during this period (see Figure 2.9) were exceptionally strong, nearing 20 per cent per annum (for unleveraged investors and significantly higher for those who had borrowed to invest) in both 2004 and 2005. This happened despite the UK economy having been relatively subdued for some time.

In 2006 the UK economy showed renewed strength for the first time in perhaps five years leading to a surprise interest rate increase in summer 2006. For the leveraged private investor the combination of yield compression and rising interest rates has the effect of reducing the level of acceptable leverage they can deploy and ultimately creates a negative yield gap (where the initial yield on a property is lower than the rate of interest).

Figure 2.9: Returns from UK Commercial Property 2001–2007

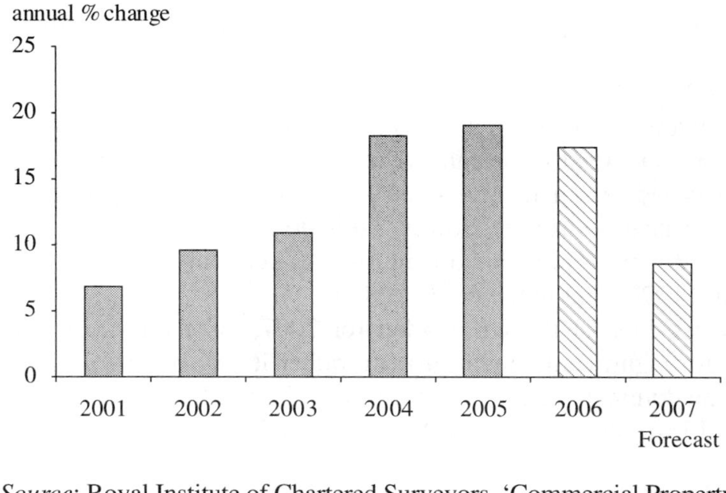

Source: Royal Institute of Chartered Surveyors, 'Commercial Property Forecasts 2006–7', <http://www.rics.org/NR/rdonlyres/BBE42F21-B8B1-4825-8918-5A998FB6614B/0/commercial_forecast0406.doc>, accessed 18/11/2006.

Table 2.4: Components of Returns in the UK Commercial Property Market 2001–2007

	Annual % change, unless stated otherwise						
	2001	2002	2003	2004	2005	2006*	2007*
Commercial property rents	3.4	−0.8	−1.6	2.3	2.7	3.4	3.7
Commercial property capital values	0.1	2.6	3.9	11.4	12.8	11.8	3.9
Commercial property yields, %	7.9	7.6	7.3	6.6	6.0	5.4	5.5
Commercial property total return	6.8	9.6	10.9	18.3	19.1	17.4	8.6

* RICS forecast
Source: Royal Institute of Chartered Surveyors, 'Commercial Property Forecasts 2006–7', <http://www.rics.org/NR/rdonlyres/BBE42F21-B8B1-4825-8918-5A998FB6614B/0/commercial_forecast0406.doc>, accessed 18/11/2006.

Such circumstances point to the easy money having been made in the UK for private investors.

The key variable for investors in the UK commercial market from this juncture will be the pace of rental growth, a more direct function of the strength of the UK economy and the pace of supply in commercial property. The Royal Institute of Chartered Surveyors forecasts that the pace of rental growth may be on an upward trend. However it is unlikely to compensate sufficiently for the fall off in yield compression. In fact in real terms rents had been in decline since 2000, falling almost 9 per cent in real terms from peak to trough. However this downward tend was much less pronounced than in previous downturns (40 per cent downturn was seen in the mid 1970s and in the early 1990s).

When we look at the UK market for 2007, most forecasters are not looking for significant capital growth, rather it will be rental yields that will be the dominant element. We can see this is in the estimates made by the Royal Institute of Chartered Surveyors in Table 2.4.

UK Residential

UK economic growth in recent years was driven by household and government spending. Household spending in turn was supported by low

2.5. Property – The World's Greatest Asset or Smoke and Mirrors?

inflation and high levels of borrowing. As the UK cut rates between 2001–2 and again in 2003–4 the economy continued to be buoyed up.

However the impact of these stimuli inevitably slowed and its economy slowed sharply from mid 2004–2006. The UK residential market responded in kind. The price increases of 26 per cent, 16 per cent, and 15 per cent slowed to 4 per cent in 2005. By September 2006 it had picked up again somewhat with an annual rate of gain back to circa 6 per cent.

The USA

The USA presents a similar story but in many ways an utterly different experience of property investing. Other than its being the most developed, highly liquid market in the world, it also comes with an abundance of land and little physical impact from the conflicts of the twentieth century. And as ever, the only thing that really divides us is language!

American Residential

Like a lot things stateside, 'big' is probably the best word to describe the US residential 'real estate' market (to use the vernacular). In common with much of the developed world the real estate market in the US has contributed very significantly to the household wealth of that country. Driven by falling interest rates since 2000 and a plentiful supply of mortgage debt ($3tn in 2003) the US residential market had created enormous wealth for individuals – in fact one estimate from 2002 suggested that residential real estate values exceeded the total value of corporate equity by some 30 per cent in the US. This is underpinned by the most advanced mortgage market on the planet with a vast secondary mortgage market. Indeed the US mortgage debt is now almost twice the size of its much talked of Federal debt.

The importance of the housing market to the general welfare of the US economy can be seen from the fact that it accounts for some one fifth of US GDP (14 per cent from direct house-building and 5–7 per cent from home improvement, appliances and furniture). Indeed it is argued by proponents of the property market that the 'home equity wealth effect' is about three times more important than the effect that the stock market has on a typical US household's wealth. Some point to this as the reason why the US consumer effectively shrugged off the stock market collapse of

2000–2002. While they didn't enjoy seeing their portfolios heading south, the continued strength in the real estate market served to buffer their household wealth and helped them maintain a consumer boom despite the largest wealth losses in generations.

The aggregate appreciation of US residential over the past decade, in common with its Irish cousin, has been spectacular. The fear much talked of in the US, is that this has grown at such a pace that it had reached bubble characteristics (we're not the only country that fixates about property prices!). The slow down in aggregate US residential price growth can be seen very clearly in Figure 2.10, suggesting that the market in many regions is seeing quite negative returns.

A simple average rate of change for the market in the US is 4.4 per cent – not very far removed from its long-term GDP growth over the same period.

In the US, there is a recognition that there are signs of price bubbles as measured by the ratio of home prices to rents (about 15 per cent higher than they were in 1991) and the home price to income ratio (about 20 per cent higher than it was in 1991). However they contend that rising house prices were justified as the level of supply coming into the market had left

Figure 2.10: Home Price Growth

Source: National Association of Realtors, 'Current and Future Real Estate Trends', <http://www.realtor.org/gapublic.nsf/files/realestatetrends.ppt/$FILE/ realestatetrends.ppt>, accessed 4/11/2006.

2.5. Property – The World's Greatest Asset or Smoke and Mirrors?

significant pent-up demand. Nonetheless price growth dropped dramatically in 2006 and many areas registered price drops for the first time in years.

Equally interestingly, the US markets that have shown the most dramatic bursts of price appreciation are, in common with Ireland, the ones that have the highest proportion of new jobs being created. So, contrary to the doomsayers' view, both the US and Ireland could, it can be argued, be characterised as quite efficient markets, in which price has reacted to demand exceeding supply as economic growth acted as a spur to property prices. Indeed, in a report in August 2000, the Bank for International Settlements argued 'even the spectacular growth in the Irish residential market appears to be in line with GDP growth'. Of note, increased supply and interest rate increases in both markets will also be the brake on price appreciation.

With more recent prices cooling significantly, the US investor accepts that there had been a bubble in residential housing and the Fed's efforts to cool the market have undoubtedly achieved a relatively gentle reduction in exuberance. Figure 2.11 shows how much the appetite for residential investment had been increasing in the US with investment in residential property hitting levels not seen since the 1950s. It is highly probable that the next chart we see will show a downturn in this percentage.

Figure 2.11: US Residential Investment as a Share of GDP

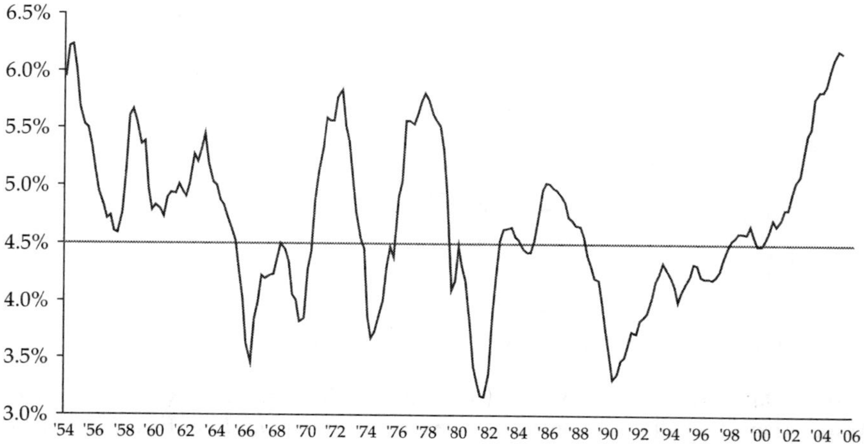

Source: Moodys/Economy.com/AEW 2006.

In *Irrational Exuberance* Robert Shiller, who predicted the demise of the stock market in the Internet bubble with such prescience, also forewarned of the risks in the US residential market – and for that matter the global residential property market. In the most recent edition of *Irrational Exuberance*, he criticises glib rationales for price increases in residential property, arguing that neither population growth nor the increase in construction costs can justify the rapid increase in prices. He argues also that even low interest rates are only a minor contributor to the price appreciation. Rather, he contends that speculation and fear of being left behind both in the US and internationally has been the driver of property prices.

American Commercial

As can be seen from Figure 2.12, the US commercial property market has been an impressive performer in recent times. The commercial market shouldn't be confused with what has been happening in residential in particular because of the level of institutional investor interest.

Figure 2.12: The US Commercial Market – A Recent Perspective

Quarterly % rate of return in US Commercial property 2001–2006

Source: David Lereah (2006), 'The Commercial Real Estate Market', National Association of Realtors, Economic Issues and Commercial Real Estate Business Trends Forum, Washington DC, <http://www.realtor.org/Research.nsf/files/06MYMComm.ppt/$FILE/06MYMComm.ppt>, accessed 18/11/2006.

2.5. Property – The World's Greatest Asset or Smoke and Mirrors?

Given the scale of the US commercial real estate market it's somewhat of a misnomer to talk about it as though it were one market. It is as diverse and complex as anything we see in polyglot, multi-currency Europe.

That said, there are certain characteristics or perhaps caricatures that set it apart. Until quite recently and in contrast to Europe, much of the property returns in the US were differentiated somewhat by the level of rental yield, with yields typically slightly higher than we have in Europe – perhaps a legacy of not being burdened with centuries of title complexities and limitations on land usage!

More recently, however, yield compression has also featured on the other side of the Atlantic. The early 2000s in US commercial office property featured a comparatively high vacancy rate (16.3 per cent in 2002, 16.5 per cent in 2003, 16.3 per cent in 2004), falling rents (−12.5 per cent in 2002, −4 per cent in 2003 and +1.4 per cent in 2004) and a reduction in supply (135m square feet in 2001, 96m square feet in 2002, 59m in 2003 and 43m in 2004). Yet despite this apparent weakness in the market itself, investors continued to invest heavily, a reflection perhaps of a switch in asset preference in particular by institutional investors. The weak property fundamentals were more than compensated for by the strength engendered through lowering interest rates and sustained strong economic performance in the early 2000s. The 'jobless recovery' that many economists spoke of during this period is what has perhaps contributed to the high but stable vacancy rates seen in the US commercial sector. 2005 saw a turnaround in fundamentals. Vacancy rates in the office sector fell to around 13 per cent with some expecting it to reach 11 per cent in 2006 and rental growth at 4.4 per cent looks reasonably strong.

The industrial sector also featured high vacancy rates (11.7 per cent in 2004, 10.1 per cent in 2003, 10 per cent in 2002) but levels fell back in 2005 to approximately 10 per cent. Rents in the sector were slipping modestly until 2005 saw growth of 2.2 per cent. In common with office space, investors were attracted into industrial space because of low interest rates and a strong economy, both of which made financing straightforward and tenants reliable. Strong supply in industrial space may constrain it.

The retail sector through this period was the most robust of the US commercial sectors as the consumer sailed through the mini-downturn of 2000–1, courtesy of their credit card providers, and maintained a consumer boom despite the softening of the US economy. This kept demand for retail space from investors and from the real estate investment trusts strong through this period.

All of this has led US 'cap rate' ('yields' in our language) to fall over the recent past.

In common with Ireland, the 'cap rates/yields' on multifamily/apartments tell a story of rising prices and exceptional returns to investors.

2005 saw a record number of commercial transactions in the US with office building sales up 30 per cent, industrial buildings up 70 per cent, retail buildings up 10 per cent and multi-family (apartments) up 63 per cent.

In summary, the commercial real estate market in the US went through a significant adjustment in the mini-recession, 2001–2003. With the equity market ravaging investor portfolios it might have been expected that investors would have rapidly sought out another asset. However, vacancy rates for office space increased significantly and rents fell substantially in more direct response to the slowing economy than to investor preferences.

By 2005, as the US economy had rebounded strongly, vacancy rates fell and rental growth returned to the market, with offices being the strongest of US performers. This trend continued in 2006 with the office vacancy rate declining again (see Table 2.5). Declining vacancy rates have fed growth in rental levels. US property investors saw significant gains and capital has queued up to participate. The downside has been that it is ever more competitive and the queues have become even longer with some suggesting that the overhang in capital is going to take some three years to deploy.

Nonetheless, the US once again has shown itself to be a very efficient market and pricing has adjusted to the economic circumstances of renewed growth making it far from certain that commercial property will be any more attractive on the other side of the Atlantic. What the US does offer Irish investors is greater depth and choice.

Despite the adjustment in pricing that has taken place, there remain some very powerful trends at play in the US.

Residential property had boomed in the US and most commentators now agree that it has peaked with some arguing for a substantial correction. However there are demographic trends at play over the longer term that will provide greater support in some markets. Florida, for example, despite its infamous historic bubble, will see a significant growth in population as

2.5. Property – The World's Greatest Asset or Smoke and Mirrors?

Table 2.5: US Commercial Property Rental Changes and Vacancy Rates

	Retail Rate Change				Vacancy Rates			
	Office	Industrial	Multi-Family	Retail	Office	Industrial	Multi-Family	Retail
2000	13.8%	9.8%	7.4%	4.9%	8.6%	6.6%	4.2%	N/A
2001	−7.2%	−0.7%	3.5%	1.9%	14.2%	9.8%	4.6%	N/A
2002	−8.3%	−4.1%	0.5%	1.4%	16.5%	11.0%	5.5%	N/A
2003	−6.7%	−4.1%	−0.3%	2.3%	16.8%	11.6%	6.4%	8.1%
2004	0.4%	−0.6%	1.5%	3.3%	15.4%	10.9%	6.2%	7.5%
2005	4.4%	2.2%	2.7%	4.0%	13.0%	10.0%	5.1%	7.2%
2006	4.4%	2.7%	3.0%	4.0%	11.3%	9.3%	5.0%	7.1%

Source: NAR, Torto Wheaton Research, reproduced in National Association of Realtors (2005) *National Association of Realtors Profile of Real Estate Markets: the United States of America,* <http://www.realtor.org/Research.nsf/files/US%20RE%20Profile%202005.pdf/$FILE/US%20RE%20Profile%202005.pdf>, accessed 27/11/2006.

the 'baby-boomers' retire to the sun (predicted to double by 2040). The populations of other states such as New York and California are forecast to fall significantly. In general the US demographics provide some level of support for the housing market although, with growth in housing stock at a twenty-five year high by 2005, it would be brave to predict much more than stability for some and losses for others. Suffice to say the bears in US residential are in the ascendancy.

Commercial property, which was worst hit around 2000–2002 has arguably seen improvements in both vacancy rates and much greater absorption and, while pricing has become more challenging as yield compression hit home, there remain reasons to be optimistic, not least that corporate America continues to surprise.

Japan – Lessons from the Recent Past

Probably the most notorious of the price collapses in property markets came in Japan in 1990, beginning at roughly the same time that its stock market collapsed in a dramatic fashion (see Figure 2.13).

Figure 2.13: Japanese Equity and Land Prices 1985–2001

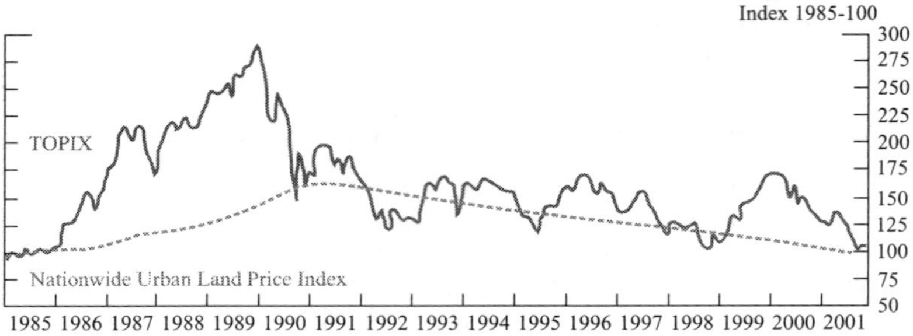

Source: Alan G. Ahearne *et al.* (2002) 'Preventing Deflation: Lessons from Japan's Experience in the 1990s', *Board of Governors of the Federal Reserve System International Finance Discussion Papers*, No. 729, June 2002, <http://www.federalreserve.gov/Pubs/ifdp/2002/729/ifdp729.pdf>, accessed 4/11/2006.

In keeping with most precedents, the property deflation was not as fast or dramatic as the stock market, but it continued for a full decade nonetheless. Ultimately it destroyed just as much wealth, with commercial land prices down 85 per cent from their 1991 peak and Japanese banks left holding huge tracts of land from defaulting borrowers (the release onto the market of which would have accelerated the price deflation).

The Japanese, in common with most developed countries, have a high level of home ownership (it stood at 60.3 per cent in 1998). The residential market also fell during this period, although not at anything like the scale of the commercial market. Nonetheless house values fell by one-third, leaving many homeowners facing negative equity, with one estimate suggesting they had collectively lost value of up to $884bn.

Ireland

Dublin in the 1990s – One of the Top Three Investments on the Planet

In their 'Rising Urban Stars' report property consultants Jones Lang LaSalle pointed out that Dublin City was amongst the three biggest winning cities

2.5. Property – The World's Greatest Asset or Smoke and Mirrors?

of the last decade. It ranked up there with Dubai and Las Vegas in terms of relative physical growth over the period of 1991–2000. While I can't be sure that there aren't other fantastical returns tucked away in various nooks and crannies of the global real estate market, I suspect that there are very few that can compete.

In this report Jones Lang LaSalle argued that all three of these cities had created an attractive business-operating environment in terms of regulation, taxation, labour flexibility and infrastructure, which had led to high levels of inward investment and immigration. A proactive city government together with a dynamic leisure and tourism industry have also helped to establish their high profile on the international stage.[13]

This was an extraordinary decade indeed both for residential and commercial markets in Dublin and the rest of Ireland. However, that, as they say, is history.

These days Dublin/Ireland is placed among the wealthiest and most developed of property markets in the world and at this stage is some way down the league table in terms of property fundamentals. We need only compare where rental yields and vacancy rates now lie to see how far our local economy has come.

As an investment class, it was hard to beat Irish residential historically. Looking forward it looks most unlikely that investors will be seeing returns of anything like the magnitude of gains seen in the past decade and, while I believe that a soft landing is the most likely outcome for the market, low yields and rising interest rates won't make for a winning combination.

Property in Your Portfolio

Most Irish investors are accustomed to thinking of commercial property investing in two camps: the buy-and-hold approach to property – the so-called 'dry investment' where you are mostly concerned with the yield, quality of tenant covenant and the building itself – and development investing, where the concern is about building and letting from start to completion. In short these approaches are either end of the spectrum of risk and return.

In between are opportunities to become involved in the so-called 'core-plus' and 'enhancement' areas. It is good advice when building the property component of your portfolio to keep these groups in mind.

Figure 2.14: Property Investment Strategies and Possible Returns to Leveraged Investors

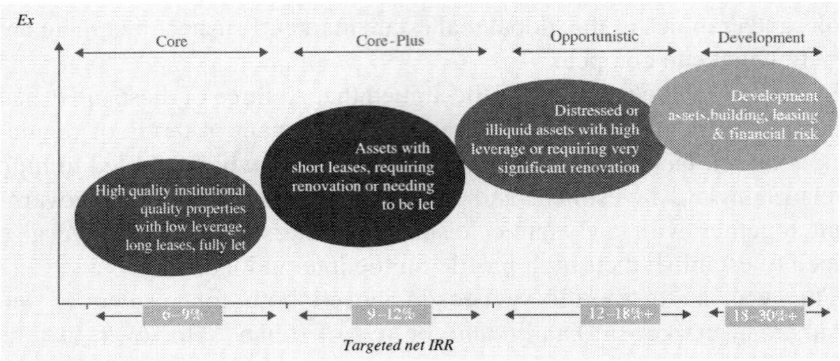

Core — High quality institutional quality properties with low leverage, long leases, fully let (6–9%)

Core-Plus — Assets with short leases, requiring renovation or needing to be let (9–12%)

Opportunistic — Distressed or illiquid assets with high leverage or requiring very significant renovation (12–18%+)

Development — Development assets, building, leasing & financial risk (18–30%+)

Targeted net IRR

Source: Adapted from JP Morgan Asset Management. Returns are indicative only.

Figure 2.14 describes how these various types of property investment fit on the 'risk/return' scale.

Right now, yield compression and rising interest rates have made the core box more challenging to deliver. Leveraged investors facing significant competition from the unleveraged buyer (pension funds) will find it increasingly challenging in most major developed markets and returns will correspondingly fall.

Property in your Wider Portfolio

In a paper published in 2003 by S. Hudson-Wilson *et al.* in the *Journal of Portfolio Management*,[14] the authors evaluated how much property an investor should have in a portfolio and why and concluded that a risk-averse investor, concerned with capital preservation, should have a quarter (23 per cent to be precise) of their portfolio in property. The reasons they cited were:

- property's track record of producing better risk adjusted (albeit lower) returns than either bonds or stocks;
- its natural tendency to act as a hedge against inflation;

2.5. Property – The World's Greatest Asset or Smoke and Mirrors?

- its particular attractiveness for investors attempting to meet a specific liability.

They cite a limitation in that the size of the asset class is dwarfed by the bond and equity markets; one can infer that not all investors will be able to reach such allocation levels.

In a more recent paper published by JP Morgan Asset Management,[15] the allocation recommended is between 10 and 15 per cent, which they contend would result in a reallocation of €1tn if all investors pursued this strategy!

The catalyst for the reallocation of capital back towards the property market was the same secular trend that underpins so much of what has happened in global markets for the past two decades. The disinflationary forces that have been at work since 1981–2 have seen a continued fall in interest rates. As rates fell, the assets that saw the most immediate and substantial adjustments were the bond and equity markets. Investors reacted accordingly and increased allocations to these assets. Towards the end of the 1990s, as the limits in valuation were reached by both, attention shifted and the first decade of this century saw property take to the vanguard. The trough in bond yields generated by loosening of the US Fed monetary policy in the early 2000s created a swath of liquidity and capacity for leverage. With the one remaining asset class that could provide a positive yield gap, property – in particular leveraged property investing – has driven property yields the way of bonds before them. The resulting returns are outlined in Table 2.6.

However one huge factor upon which all of the gains in property can be maintained is the sheer weight of private and institutional capital supporting the property market globally. From a position in 2001 in which less than $200 billion was flowing into the property market, capital inflows into property markets were over twice that amount by 2006. In part a consequence of global economic growth and in part a mathematical consequence of lower interest rates, the most obvious risk is that the easy money in property has been made. Nonetheless, even the most 'Cassandric' of commentators are unlikely to dismiss the weight of capital as a potential bulwark against a market decline.

Table 2.6: Commercial Property Price Appreciation 2002–2005

	2002	2003	2004	2005
US	6.8	9.0	14.5	18.0
UK	9.6	10.9	18.3	19.1
Netherlands	8.8	7.1	7.8	10.2
Sweden	2.4	0.9	5.8	12.7
Finland	5.7	5.9	5.6	7.4
France	8.6	8.1	10.1	15.2
Germany	3.9	2.9	1.1	0.5
Ireland	2.3	12.7	11.5	24.3
Hong Kong*	−11.0	10.0	62.7	51.9
Singapore*	−16.7	−10.7	4.2	4.2

* Office market only and price appreciation only
Source: NCREIF, IPD, CBRE, Singapore Urban Redevelopment Authority, Datastream and Bank of Ireland Private Banking 2006.

Direct and Indirect Investment

Another feature of the property market that is likely to come to the fore for investors is the question of whether it is more efficient to invest directly (i.e. buy a single property itself) or more indirectly through pooled vehicles.

Curiously investors tend to find it more difficult to dispassionately evaluate which approach is better, despite clear reasons for each. The lure of the 'touch and feel' of owning one individual property tends to cloud rationality and investor objectivity.

In his paper 'Is direct investment in international property markets justifiable?'[16] Patrick McAllister of the University of Reading outlines some of the principal differences which should prove instructive to investors facing such a dilemma:

1. *Diversification as the Primary Motivation*

Most international property investment is motivated by a desire to diversify as investors seek higher yields and potentially higher returns than are available domestically and in the case of corporate investors to match local liabilities. As it requires immense resources to develop a globally diversified portfolio, indirect forms of investment tend to be favoured. Additionally, as

2.5. Property – The World's Greatest Asset or Smoke and Mirrors?

investors who are endeavouring to diversify are seeking out property that is non-correlated with the equity and bond markets, there can be difficulty with assessing the extent to which this can be achieved through direct investment. McAllister cites evidence of the property markets in Hong Kong, Singapore and Australia being highly correlated with equity markets whereas the US, Germany and Holland demonstrate low correlation.

2. *Information Costs*

The 'dumb foreigner' effect is widely recognised by international property investors, in particular in markets where there is dearth of public information or knowledge. Indeed evidence that McAllister cites in his paper points to lower returns being achieved by foreign investors than domestic investors, supporting the idea that the dumb foreigner is better served investing alongside locals.

3. *Management Costs*

The question of costs will cut both ways. Funds, and in particular funds of funds, will appear expensive at first glance to the investors. However, direct property investment comes with both high entry barriers for individual investors and additional management costs. Arguably large fund management companies benefit from economies of scale (as evidenced by the consolidation of the REIT industry in the US).

4. *Transaction Costs*

Transaction costs will also vary enormously. There are some arguments that contend that some of the company-based arrangements for transacting property are more cost-effective.

5. *Liquidity*

Property always suffers from illiquidity. It is one of the strongest reasons why investors must demand a higher premium on their property investments than on more liquid investments such as bonds or even shares. Direct investing is probably the more illiquid form with no ready secondary market in which to transact.

Indirect forms of investment such as property funds provide a reasonable level of liquidity and semi-direct investment such as property syndicates tend to provide a relatively low level.

6. *Performance Measurement*

Property performance measurement is difficult at the best of times and many researchers in the area contend that the values we see in indices are too 'smooth' because they represent estimates by the owners – who naturally won't want to display losses too publicly. The belief is that the result reveals an under-estimation of volatility in property prices and a lag in market valuations. This can create a misleadingly positive read on the risk/return/correlation characteristics of the asset class and is arguably more pronounced with direct investment.

Property Syndicates

Property syndicates as a form of property investing have become an increasingly important part of Irish investors' property portfolios, in particular as a means of diversifying internationally.

Typically such arrangements are vehicles whose value moves in accordance with real property values. Syndications are usually completed via co-ownership agreement or through company structures and typically involve a consortium of investors numbering from fifteen to fifty investors. Alongside investor equity, a bank will usually finance the vehicle on a non-recourse basis to the investors and the syndicate will purchase the property. Most syndicates are intended to last for a period of seven to eight years and tend to be quite illiquid.

Geared Property Funds

Available from most life assurance companies and investment houses, geared property funds in many ways resemble property syndicates insofar as they too gather equity from a pool of investors and then 'gear' the exposure with bank finance. Many geared property funds offer a diversified selection of properties within the portfolio, something not generally done by syndicates.

2.5. Property – The World's Greatest Asset or Smoke and Mirrors?

Diversified Un-geared Property Funds

Also available from most of the life companies are the traditional pooled funds that simply purchase a diversified number of properties without using gearing.

A Pause for Thought

If one stands back from the ebb and flow of the property market, and even the markedly different characteristics of the individual markets, one aspect stands out for these developed markets – the same disinflationary environment that generated a fall in interest rates over the last two decades has prompted periods where the yield gap has been substantial and consequently capital, particularly leveraged private capital, has found its way into the property market. Such a period has been immensely supportive of the types of returns achieved by investors in the past decade, most particularly in the world-beating Irish market.

Predicting the Next Dublin

The cities that will generate the big returns of the future cannot of course be predicated with any certainty but there are themes that many in this field point to. Jones Lang LaSalle's 2003 study 'Rising Urban Stars – Uncovering Future Winners' suggests three 'thematic' categories that are worth considering:

1. *Technology-driven*

Jones Lang LaSalle suggest that cities such as Helsinki, Austin and Raleigh-Durham, cities that are already technology rich, will continue to flourish and cities such as Bangalore, Budapest, Dalian, San José, Suzhou and Tallinn will emerge in coming years as technological hubs.

2. *Environment-driven*

They suggest that cities that will flourish as they enhance their environment include mature metropolises such as Barcelona, Cape Town, SE Queensland (includes Brisbane), Copenhagen, Calgary and Port Alegre.

3. Local Economy-driven

Jones Lang La Salle point to cities where economic growth will be a support to price rises and suggest that second line cities such as Chongqing and Xian will be the type to benefit most.

There are of course many such lists and different criteria for success but what is suggested is that one needs to understand what will drive a city's growth in the fashion that drove Dublin (inward investment, low tax and skilled workforce did it for Dublin, in case you need reminding!). Other researchers point to the emerging cities of the Pacific Rim, or the value to be had in regional cities in the big developed Western European and Scandinavian markets or to the demographics that will push certain US cities and not others.

Property investing will remain a very considerable feature of Irish investment preferences for a considerable time to come, in no small part as other asset classes have displayed much greater volatility over the past generation. The property sector will inevitably see some years of poor performance especially as capital in this sector becomes increasingly mobile and moves in a manner more akin to other capital markets. Nonetheless, the ability to gear, to obtain higher levels of yield and to capitalise on yield gaps as they emerge will make property attractive in many parts of the world.

Asia – The 'Newest' Property Market cannot be Ignored

Take one part demographic dividend, one part technological enablement, cook with explosive economic growth, sprinkle this with an emergent middle class and stew for a couple of decades in undervalued currency. These are both the risks and opportunities presented in many of the rapidly expanding property markets of Asia.

Even a cursory glance at initial yields in most Asian property markets is enough to make Irish investors sit up and take note. Figure 2.15 shows the low vacancy rates and a premium on yields when compared to Europe and should be just the combination the private (geared) investor requires. However, buyer beware – utterly different legal and lease arrangements, volatile currencies and geopolitical risk present significant question marks for investors that simply don't apply nearer to home.

Figure 2.15: Asian Property Yields and Vacancy Rates, Year End 2005

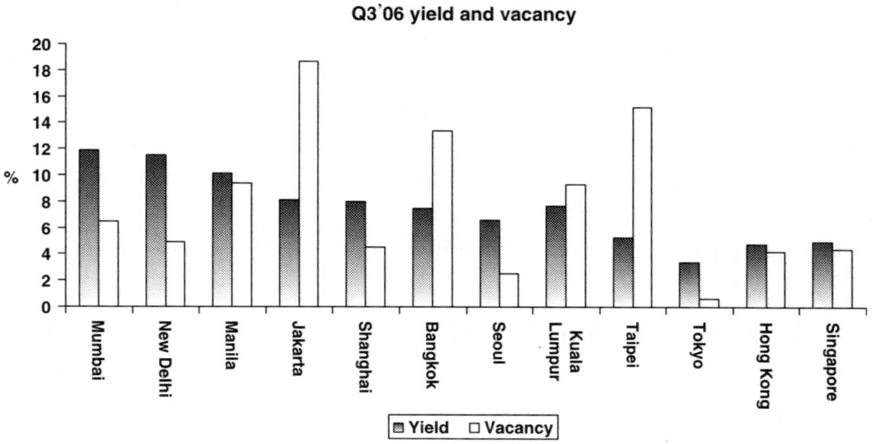

Q3'06 yield and vacancy

(Bar chart showing Yield and Vacancy percentages for: Mumbai, New Delhi, Manila, Jakarta, Shanghai, Bangkok, Seoul, Kuala Lumpur, Taipei, Tokyo, Hong Kong, Singapore)

Source: Bank of Ireland Private Banking 2006.

Take-Away Advice

It's hard in 2006 to make as strong a case for Irish and indeed UK property investment when compared to alternatives, with yields comparatively low and borrowing costs rising. There's less danger of a price correction than many Cassandric commentators assert, given the sheer scale of economic growth and demographically and commercially driven demand, but the double digit returns are behind us.

To generate returns of the kind we've seen in the past decade will necessitate taking either a riskier investment or a more active role in its management in core-plus and enhancement areas.

For a better chance of a positive yield gap with limited risk, look to the western shores of the EU (with better value, little currency risk, but plenty of tax nuances).

For investors prepared to move further out the risk curve, the US may present little more by way of either vacancy or yield but its economy may be capable of greater growth. Stay away from most of the residential market (barring multi-family) and be prepared to get in a queue for the commercial market.

> The developing European economies, particularly the recent accession states provide some uplift in yield at present (though not as much as one might hope) and continue to offer some degree of 'convergence' play. However don't expect every part of Eastern Europe to follow Ireland's path in like form; they are not the same and few will have a decade like we just did. Don't ignore the Far East, the yields are better, the economies on a high growth trajectory and in all probability investors will be well served by taking an interest in countries such as India and Korea.

2.6. Bonds – Europe and the US, a Tale of Two Continents

The bond market is a simply colossal part of the global financial markets and there is no getting away from it when it comes to managing your personal finances. It's not too straightforward and as a consequence tends not to make the same headlines that other assets do, but don't let that detract from its importance.

Scale of Global Bond Markets

In 2004 the IAPF (Irish Association of Pension Funds) estimated that the size of the global bond market runs to some $45 trillion, making it probably the most important part of the global capital markets.

The most significant component of the global bond market is the US bond market. Looked at from the perspective of government, quasi-government and corporate funding, US bonds account for roughly 47.6 per cent of bonds in issuance around the world. Add in the highly developed US mortgage-backed and other asset-backed securities along with money markets and the figure can increase further. Suffice to say, this is much bigger than the property market.

With the decreasing role that governments play in modern economies when compared to the scale of government that prevailed twenty years ago, the mix between government and corporate debt in the overall bond market has also changed significantly. As government's role declined relatively, companies have issued increasingly more debt as lower interest rates made the capital markets a cheap place to fund their businesses.

2.6. Bonds – Europe and the US, a Tale of Two Continents

Given that the prevailing weight of argument now tilts to small government and prudent management of borrowing we can expect bond markets to become increasingly more North American in form in the years to come.

In the US – the most developed of the bond markets – mortgage related debt is the largest sector, accounting for over a quarter of the market, with corporate debt making up about a fifth. In the EU the market is dominated by government debt which accounts for 60 per cent of bonds in issuance compared to 29 per cent for corporates and 11 per cent for mortgage-backed.

Principal Bond Types

The bond market consists of a vast array of different securities, sufficiently varied and complex to merit a library of their own. So any description contained in two to three pages is necessarily incomplete. However it is important to know that the variety in which they are available makes for colossal differences in risks and potential returns; hence this short diversion into 'bonds for beginners'.

Government Bonds

As the name suggests, government bonds are debt instruments issued by sovereign states. A government may issue bonds in its national bond market or indeed in the Eurobond market or the foreign sector of an overseas bond market.

The government bonds issued by the US Government are typically seen as the nearest thing in global markets to the risk-free rate. The US market splits into three broad 'fixed principal' categories (where capital is repaid of a fixed nominal value in the future): Treasury bills, Treasury notes and Treasury bonds. Treasury bills, the shortest of the three, are discount instruments, where the return to the investor is the difference between the price at purchase and the maturity/face value. Securities issued with a maturity date greater than one year and less than ten years are called Treasury notes. Those with maturities greater than ten years are called Treasury bonds (though these are no longer being issued by the US). To varying degrees sovereign governments have some version of this. German *Bunds* typically have maturities from eight to thirty years, whereas their notes tend to be less than five years. In Italy the Government issues bonds, *Buoni del Tesoro Poliennali* or BTPs, which provide fixed rate coupons over five, ten and thirty years; *Certificati di credito del Tesoro*, which are seven-year floating rate notes; and two year zero coupons called CTZs. The French issue long-dated bonds called OATs (*Obligation Assimilable du Trésor*) over terms of up to thirty years and notes called BTANs (*Bons du Trésor à Taux Fixe et à Intérêt Annuel*) with terms between two and five years. The list can go on and comes with a host of wonderful acronyms.

Inflation-linked bonds
In some jurisdictions, it has also become practice to issue inflation-linked bonds, such as Treasury Inflation Protected Securities (TIPS) in the USA, or in France where there are inflation-linked bonds amongst the OATs recently issued, or in Australia where a significant portion of the government bonds in issue are 'Treasury Indexed Bonds'.

Inflation-linked bonds are far from being just an interesting curiosity and are finding their way into a lot of discussions within the investment industry as to the role they can play. They work as follows: the Government issues a bond with a fixed coupon rate – this is the rate that the investor ultimately earns above the rate of inflation. The 'principal amount' is the amount that the Government uses to rebase both the amount of the coupon in euros or dollars and maturity value, thereby inflation-protecting both the income and capital returned by the bond. Of course, investors in such securities pay for these handsome features with a much lower coupon. Why they have become so interesting of late is due to a belief that they will repay investors handsomely if inflation returns in unforeseen measure. In contrast to conventional bonds, which can be so badly impacted by inflation, TIPs or Inflation protected OATs may benefit from such conditions.

Strips
Zero coupon bonds are discount bonds under which an investor receives no cash flows, just a repayment of a fixed principal over a fixed period of time. Most particularly in the US, demand for long-dated zero coupon bonds and an absence of issuance by the Government, led the investment industry to create 'Strips', a repackaging of government securities enabling the delivery of risk-free zero coupon bonds over longer periods of time.

2.6. Bonds – Europe and the US, a Tale of Two Continents

Semi-Government Bonds

In many parts of the world, the debt of semi-state entities, regional governments, and government agencies is funded through the issuance of bonds. The US, again, provides us with the most developed market of this kind, in particular in the mortgage market where there are two government agencies issuing securities to help the market for capital for homeowners: the Federal National Mortgage Association (Fannie Mae) and the Federal Home Loan Mortgage Corporation (Freddie Mac). There are also agencies in the US issuing securities based on farmers (Farmer Mac) and students (Sallie Mae)!

These are of interest to investors everywhere because of the type of securities that they create. Mortgage pass-through securities, for instance, are securities created from a pool of mortgage holders, whose principal and interest payments are pooled together. The investment characteristics of what can be made available to investors from a wide pool of investors is vast.

Consider what might be available if a firm had the cashflows from, say, 5,000 mortgages arriving in every month. The entity issuing the 'collateralised mortgage obligation' or CMO might choose to provide the first tranche of investors with a high level of security – so they might get paid a lower coupon than is coming in from the mortgage pool but be insulated from the risk of individuals defaulting on or pre-paying the debt. Conversely they might provide some investors at the other end of the risk scale with a very high level of coupon but ask them to absorb a much higher level of default (the most extreme versions are sometimes nicknamed 'nuclear waste' given their inherently unstable nature!).

As you might imagine this is a complex and risky part of the mortgage market, where investors should take special care.

Corporate Debt Securities

Companies everywhere look to borrow. Typically it happens in one of two fashions – either from a bank, or directly from the capital markets by issuing debt. Broadly speaking, the debt securities that companies issue come in the following forms: corporate bonds, medium-term notes, commercial paper and asset-backed securities.

Corporate Bonds, Medium-Term Notes and Commercial Paper

Corporate bonds are simply debt instruments issued by corporate entities in a fixed amount. They come in either secured or unsecured form, with the former being less risky for investors. Most major issuers will be given a credit rating by one of the major agencies such as Standard & Poors, Fitch or Moodys. The higher the rating, the less likely that the issuer will default. Nonetheless corporate bonds are typically considered of higher risk than high-quality sovereign debt. Medium-term notes are debt securities continuously offered by the issuer; despite their name they can have terms ranging from one to thirty years. Commercial paper takes the form of unsecured promissory notes, backed only by the promise of the issuing corporation, typically having a term of less than one year.

Asset-Backed Securities

Asset backed securities are a wide class of bonds in which the repayments promised are backed by a pool of assets which may include car loans, personal loans, credit cards, mortgages, commercial assets and others. Again the US is the most advanced market in these securities but they are a prominent feature of European markets also. Corporations can be attracted to using such vehicles as it can enable them to raise funds more cheaply in an off-balance sheet fashion or it may enable them to create a higher credit rated investment for end investors.

Collateralised Debt Obligations

One of the fastest growing of the asset backed securities is the so-called collateralised debt obligation or CDO. With CDOs, an asset manager takes responsibility for the assets underlying the bond. CDOs typically issue a series of tranches of individually rated bonds which may range from AAA to junk in status. Private investors should sit up and take note as CDOs will feature in many offerings in the coming years along with many different underlyings. The method will produce a highly leveraged way for investors to access assets other than simply credit.

2.6. Bonds – Europe and the US, a Tale of Two Continents

The Risks in Bonds

After all of that, if you're still with me, you'll appreciate that the bond market is a vast and complex one, no less varied than the equity market. It also comes with an array of risks that investors should be aware of, the principal amongst which are:

Interest Rate Risk

The plain vanilla bond promises to pay out a fixed coupon and a repayment of original capital after a fixed period of time. So at its issue, if it were paying a coupon of 5 per cent in line with the prevailing interest rates, its 'yield to maturity' would be 5 per cent. However if, some months later, interest rates were to increase, then another bond issued in the market would perhaps have a coupon of 5.5 per cent, making the first bond less attractive and forcing its price down. Hence the simple inverse relationship between interest rates and bond prices – as interest rates increase, bond prices fall and vice versa.

Other factors that will 'mechanically' impact on the price of a bond include the term to maturity, the existence of call options embedded in the bond and the scale of the coupon itself (lower coupon rates mean higher sensitivity to interest rate changes).

The method that is most commonly used to measure interest rate risk is called 'duration', a mathematical approximation for estimating the responsiveness of a bond price to interest rate changes.

Yield Curve Risk

If we only had one interest rate risk with which to contend, life in the bond market would be relatively simple to master. However, the interest rate affecting a specific bond is only the first factor that must be considered. The second is typically 'yield curve risk'. The 'yield curve' is the graphical depiction of interest rates over a variety of different terms.

As investors, because we are usually dealing with more than one bond in an investor's portfolio, chances are that we'll be looking at bonds with more than one maturity. So the way interest rates alter across a range of terms is what will impact on the total portfolio. We could find a 'parallel shift' in the yield curve, under which all rates lift by the same quantum, causing all bond prices to fall. We might find that there is a 'lift in the curve at the front end and flattening at the back of the curve', which could cause short-dated bonds to fare poorly while others tread water. Or we might discover a 'yield curve inversion' (rising short rates, falling long rates such as has happened in the US in December 2005) in which shorter-dated bonds fare poorly and longer-dated bonds do rather well. Or from a flat curve one could see a 'normalising' in which short-dated bonds do well and long-dated ones do worse. Confused? You should be. Movement of the different parts of the yield curve is a very difficult area to predict with accuracy and competing economic theories are propounded as to why the yield curve is the way it is.

One tool bond investors use to gauge where we might be headed is to analyse the 'steepness' of the yield curve. In mid-2000, the curve in both the US and EU began to get steeper, reaching a peak somewhere around the start of 2003. By the middle of 2004, it had reached levels that marked it out as unusually steep, as markets predicted interest rate increases in the US and Europe. As the year came to a close, the curve began to flatten, partly as the US did make cuts and partly as Europe began to talk of not cutting (with some thinking a cut was possible). A flattening curve, despite interest rate increases, may in fact turn out to be reasonably attractive for bond investors, as was the case in 2004 in a number of markets.

However, by 2006, both the US and UK had seen yield curves flatten and to a modest degree 'invert'; a position whereby longer-dated bonds yield less than shorter-dated ones. Some contend that this is a reliable indicator that the central banks are prepared to tilt the economies into recession to stave off inflation.

Other Risks

There are a host of other risks to worry about as a bond investor, all beyond the scope of this text. Suffice to say, default, downgrade and credit spread risk, liquidity risk, exchange rate, call, event, prepayment and reinvestment risk all are matters that your average bond trader might be concerned about late at night.

Confusing Bond Funds with Bonds

A common misconception from which many investors suffer when considering bonds as an investment is to mix up the features of an individual

2.6. Bonds – Europe and the US, a Tale of Two Continents

bond with those of a bond fund. Bond funds which typically consist of a portfolio of bonds are not guaranteed in any fashion by anyone. Yes, they may have underlying bonds that come with varying levels of risk and security of repayment, but bond funds themselves do not make a promise to repay all of a person's investment at a fixed date.

Some Views on How the Bond Market Might Perform in the Current Environment

At the outset of the section on equities I outlined a view that contends we are likely to see more inflation in the global system in the years to come and that we are leaving the period of disinflation behind us. That should not be good news for bonds, in general.

Bond markets delivered strong returns to investors, on the whole, throughout the period of falling interest rates that stretched from the early 1980s until now.

The US Market

The Fed, in an effort to sustain the economic well-being of the US economy in the period after 2000, brought interest rates to levels not seen for half a century – arguably to unnaturally low levels – thereby pump-priming the US economy with cheap money, helping it to bounce gently off what might otherwise have been a significant recession in 2002–2003 and guiding it back to strong growth levels in 2004/5. By comparison to their predecessors it's easy to conclude that the Fed is just better at it now than it used to be. Fans of Mr. Greenspan argued that he had indeed 'tamed the wave' and brought a stability not heretofore seen in the business cycle. Cynics point to his legacy being an excess of credit washing around the US consumer system, which has fuelled a trade deficit, and will cause a lot of heartache once rates start finding their way back to more normal levels.

Like most debates of this kind, it is peppered by extremes but there is probably a grain of truth in both interpretations. However, what few would argue with is that the Fed has been tightening in 'measured fashion' for the past three years or so and Mr Bernanke's reign is likely to see more of the same for at least the initial period, making US Treasuries among the less likely investments to come top of the class for a while to come. Once the tightening cycle in the US turns, as it appears to have, investors from this side of the Atlantic may renew their interest in US bonds. What's just as likely to spark interest in parts of the US bond market, however, is the level of the US dollar versus the euro and other, particularly Far Eastern, currencies. 2006 saw further dollar weakness and one can, in the short term, make a case for continued dollar weakness. For the dollar to reassert itself needs some rebalancing of the trade and current account deficits and a less pegged system of exchange between the dollar and emerging markets currencies, changes which will take longer to work their way through the system.

Euroland

Up until the latter half of 2005 most mid- to long-dated European bond investors had seen a couple of years of reasonably strong returns as interest rate increases in the euro area went on the long finger. Mid-2005 to mid-2006 was a less hospitable environment as the ECB began the process of increasing interest rates. Having increased rates throughout 2006, there remains a strong possibility that the ECB will continue to raise rates. However it is unlikely we'll see a replication of the relative scale of US increases in Europe. That may make the European bond market a relatively unrewarding place to be into 2007. As neither rate cuts nor a further flattening of the curve will support the market, it will be all down to how far the ECB sees it necessary to go to dampen inflation. This is the risk for investors.

The United Kingdom

Alone in 2005, the UK looked to be finished with its monetary tightening, making it a relatively more benign environment for bond investors.

However a stronger UK economy in early 2006 sparked fears that inflationary pressures might resurface and led to a surprise increase in interest rates in August of 2006, a policy that may yet be set to continue in 2007.

Japan

Japan has been a unique case for a number of years as the Bank of Japan pursued a policy of 0% interest rates. Mid-2006 saw the Japanese abandon this policy and return to positive interest rates.

2.6. Bonds – Europe and the US, a Tale of Two Continents

Corporate Bonds

As for corporate bonds, the conventional theory is that you are taking additional risk – governments tend to go bust with less frequency than companies – but a word of caution is appropriate. Credit spreads tightened considerably over the past couple of years as investors began to believe that the business world was a less risky place. By historical standards they are at the lower end of the scale and many offer less than 1 per cent over governments. The one place that one does not want to be is in a corporate bond market with widening credit spreads. I would not give much probability to that occurring in the short term, especially with equity volatility levels so comparatively low. However if you are of bearish disposition, an environment of narrow credit spreads and low equity volatility make the potential for change one directional. The events surrounding General Motors debt being downgraded in spring of 2005 and the ensuing widening of credit spreads point to a very real lesson in why investment markets fail to maintain the perfect environment for very long.

That said, there's a portion of the corporate market (the high yield bond market – junk bonds in common parlance) that's likely to attract quite a bit of attention. The returns this sector achieved in 2003–5 attracted attention, although such returns were also a feature of the falling corporate default rates that we've seen in the early part of the decade (at the start of 2002 default rates of speculative grade bonds ran to nearly 11 per cent, by November 2006 it was down to 1.5 per cent).[17] An environment in which low grade corporate debt pays a reasonable premium and in which default rates are so low can make junk attractive and has done in 2006.

Take-Away Advice

Bond investors of many hues, including those who favoured the more conservative parts of the market, have faired well over the periods since 1980. The secular trend of disinflation supported a long decline in interest rates which in turn generated handsome returns for bonds.

Those who chose the credit markets over this long time horizon also saw outsized returns achieved as credit spreads narrowed and defaults reached historic lows.

Unfortunately that means that there's not much juice left in the bond market, probably globally.

> As a safety valve in your portfolio bonds will always have a role to play. However I don't believe that you'll see much change ahead of cash type returns in the years to come.
>
> Proponents of credit argue that it's an environment in which you've never had it so good with default rates at 10 year lows. With credit spreads at near historic lows the premium being paid for the risk of reversion to the mean in defaults seems a poor bet.

2.7. Private Equity – The New Kings of Capitalism

Private equity as an investment class is a remote and little known part of the capital markets for many investors but, in common with hedge funds, it is a field that has become much more mainstream as large financial institutions eye the returns achieved by private equity investors with considerable envy. It's a corner of the investment industry that is littered with failures but pot-marked by brilliance and outstanding returns.

Private equity investing consists primarily of:

- *Venture capital*: Venture capital or 'VC' is the financing of the creation or expansion of a small private company, most typically in high tech or emerging markets.
- *Buy-out*: Buy-outs are the financing or spin off of an established firm with a mix of debt and equity and more typically in a mature industry.
- *Mezzanine*: The thin strips of more junior debt-like finance paying significantly higher returns but facing much more equity-like risk.

The sector is characterised by low liquidity, long time horizons, periodic cash flows, substantial risk and historically high returns.

When compared to public equity investing the point is often made that the only difference is the nature of the ownership. There are however substantive differences from the investor's perspective (see Table 2.7).

The early days of private equity investing principally involved buying shares in private companies, holding them and selling them at a profit. Generally it was the preserve of wealthy families and some investment banks, and they usually confined themselves to small fast-growing business

2.7. Private Equity – The New Kings of Capitalism

Table 2.7: Comparing Private and Public Equity

	Private Equity	Public Equity
Ownership	Private Ownership: Concentrated	Public markets: Dispersed
Liquidity	Dependent on liquidity events such as buyout, IPO, and cash flows realised by PE firm	Trade daily
Fees	Management fees 1.5–2.5% p.a.; Carried interest 20–30% over 'preferred return' (typically 8% for buyout funds); Fees on uninvested funds	Management fees of 1–2% p.a.
Regulation	Private placement partnerships	Exchanges and higher level of regulation
Time to Invest	Potentially very long capital committal periods	Effectively immediate
Information	Low	High
Transparency	Low, with limited portfolio disclosure	High

sectors. By the 1980s it had developed new techniques and the infamous hostile leveraged buy-outs of this period were what cast the private equity firms in the role of villain. The highly leveraged hostile takeover is a much rarer bird these days, with most private equity firms having to raise substantial equity as well as debt. Indeed private equity firms have gone through quite a transformation from the frontiersmen of the 1980s LBOs* to the very heart of the establishment. According to a recent survey by the *Economist* magazine, 'private equity firms…plausibly define themselves as providing a safe haven in which firms can pursue long-term growth, sheltered from the short-term storms of the public stock markets…Well-known firms that have recently been 'nurtured' by private equity include Burger King, Polaroid, Universal Studios, Houghton Mifflin, BHS, Ducati Motor and the Savoy group.'[18]

So how does this industry work? There are two principal but quite distinct areas as included in the private equity industry – the buy-out funds

---

* Leveraged buy-outs

and the venture funds. According to Goldman Sachs, world-wide there are some 2,700 firms specialising in the field and, particularly as returns from public equity turned anaemic, investment interest grew amongst pensions funds, private individuals and other large investors.

US private equity houses had a bumper period in the late 1990s, early 2000s, with massive inflows, particularly into venture funded technology start-ups. In 2000, venture had their biggest ever year raising $107bn in the US alone, with buy-outs adding a further $89bn. The levels of fundraising tapered rapidly enough with the collapse of the technology bubble and in 2003 the US Venture industry raised an estimated $7bn with buy-outs raising $38bn. The number of firms and the total of actual investments committed fell back considerably as a consequence and the post-Internet bubble years were comparatively lean for the industry.

However 2005 was a resurgent bumper year for private equity fundraising with a combined global total of $227 billion raised globally.[19] This compares to $129 billion for 2004 and bears testimony to the popularity of private equity funds amongst investors. Two thirds of these funds were US based although growth in European private equity investing increased by a greater percentage.

This trend is also seen in the extent to which trade sales in the US outnumbered venture-backed IPOs,* which had become so prevalent in the late 1990s.

Venture Investing – A Tale of Two Cultures

Before progressing it is worth noting that when it comes to venture investing and comparing the US and Europe we are essentially comparing apples and oranges. Venture funds in the US are most typically comprised of experienced entrepreneurs who have run start-up businesses and who have often experienced both business failure and success (business failures are worn like medals in US boardrooms). The Americans like to provide 'value-added services' to their investments and take quite a hands-on role in their development; equally they will tend to cut and run once a firm shows signs of failing. By contrast, in Europe the venture funds are typically

---

* Initial public offerings

2.7. Private Equity – The New Kings of Capitalism

run by former bankers, consultants, accountants and lawyers whose CVs won't have a sniff of failure. They tend not to get as involved in seed capital stage investing, are hands-off in approach and focused on minimising downside risk to their investment. The two models are different with one producing stronger returns and more failures. The US model outperforms because of its focus on 'home runs' – hitting it big by finding the next Google amongst another hundred or so failed or mediocre firms. The difference in approach can be seen in the fact that, during the 1990s, there were at least eleven venture companies in the US that exited, providing investors with a return of 250 times their original capital. However, in Europe there were about ten firms that exited providing investors with a return over twenty times original capital.

Private Equity Performance Measurement

Another substantive difference for investors who first look at private equity investing is the manner in which performance is measured which is utterly different to the rate of return or IRR* type returns to which private investors are accustomed. Instead private equity firms talk about 'vintage year returns' (this truly is an industry with attitude, drawing its performance measurement lexicon directly from the vineyards of Bordeaux!).

A private equity manager will talk in terms of a 1997 vintage year performance and will quite possibly only talk about it from 2002 onwards. The reason for this is relatively straightforward but is one that makes an uncomfortable bedfellow for most private investors. Firstly, venture investing in particular will involve fund-making commitments over a period of time – not every deal will arrive at their doorstep on day one of receiving the investor's money. This 'committal period' is something to which institutional investors are quite accustomed and they tend to have less difficulty saying to a private equity firm 'yes, we're good for $5m whenever you're ready for it over the next few years.' However it can leave private equity firms with very substantial uninvested funds which for private investors can prove frustrating. Secondly, bear in mind what private equity firms term the 'J-Curve' phenomenon. The J-Curve describes the fact that a venture investment will require the private equity firm to spend money before it reaps the benefits. This will often mean hard cash being spent in

---

* Internal rate of return

the initial phases of development without the fund seeing any payback, leading to losses in net asset value in the early years.

Hence a comparison between a relatively new private equity fund and, for example, a managed equity fund probably isn't very realistic until we start talking about much older vintage private equity funds. Some argue that the first six years or so of performance give no real clue as to the final performance that will be achieved by the fund – for wine connoisseurs the parallels are appealing! For the private investor it also means being in a position to commit funds for the long term which may not always suit. Indeed some suggest that the funds launched into the post-2000 bubble period probably found more bargain basement deals than had been seen for a long time. Some of these funds may yet display extraordinary returns despite what the previous graph has to say about them thus far – what this does illustrate is that the J-Curve is a very real phenomenon.

Another curiosity that distorts the comparison of performance of private equity is a tendency amongst its advocates to point to top quartile fund performances only. While at face value this may seem a bit like pointing only to the winners, it has some basis in reality as many venture investments included in the broader indices have less commercially focused investments emanating from universities, R&D departments and government bodies. What's more instructive about this, however, is the manner in which returns are distributed amongst private equity funds. A very small number account for the lion's share of returns in this market. For instance, from 1980 to 2001 the average private equity buy-out fund generated slightly lower return than the S&P 500* with the average venture fund slightly ahead of the same index. However the top quartile of private equity funds returned 23 per cent per annum for that period – well ahead of the S&P.

Table 2.8 shows the returns achieved in the US market for various types of private equity funds and serves to underline the significant outperformance achieved by private equity over long periods.

What is striking, however, is that, taking US venture as an example, only fifteen funds accounted for about half of these returns. What that key fact tells us is that private equity will remain immensely risky. Yes, a small number produce extraordinary returns that can lay just claim to the talents of alchemists, but the industry by its nature generates losses and poor returns in even more generous servings than its hedge fund cousin.

---

* Standard & Poor's 500 – US equity market index of 500 leading US shares.

2.7. Private Equity – The New Kings of Capitalism

Table 2.8: Thomson Financials' US Private Equity Performance Index (PEPI) Investment Horizon Performance through 30 June 2006

Fund type	1 year	3 year	5 year	10 year	20 year
Early/Seed VC	11.20	5.40	−7.60	36.90	20.50
Balanced VC	20.50	12.50	−0.20	17.00	14.50
Later stage VC	16.40	9.40	−1.10	9.50	13.70
All Venture	**16.20**	**9.00**	**−3.50**	**20.80**	**16.50**
Small buyouts	12.10	9.60	3.70	7.10	25.90
Medium buyouts	21.50	11.80	5.00	11.10	16.10
Large buyouts	26.80	15.80	6.30	8.60	12.50
Mega buyouts	28.50	17.50	7.20	8.90	11.60
All buyouts	**27.30**	**16.30**	**6.60**	**8.90**	**13.40**
Mezzanine	9.70	5.30	2.60	6.20	8.70
All private equity	**22.50**	**13.40**	**3.60**	**11.40**	**14.20**
NASDAQ	5.6	10.2	0.0	6.2	11.7
S&P 500	6.6	9.2	0.7	6.6	9.79

Source: Thomson Financial/National Venture Capital Association (2006), *Private Equity Performance Show Stability in Q2 2006*, <http://www.nvca.org/pdf/Q206 Performancefinal.pdf>, accessed 5/11/06.

And not Cheap at the Price

Private equity investing is also amongst the most expensive of investment classes when it comes to paying fees. Typically the general partner (those running the show) get paid between 1.5 per cent and 2 per cent per annum in management fees as well as typically 20–30 per cent of the profits made on any investment (the so-called 'carried interest').

Increasingly both institutional and private investors are choosing to access the industry via funds of funds – specialists who get access to private equity funds and blend them together. Given the opacity involved these firms are seeing a lot of interest and are an increasingly important part of the industry; of course they will also charge their fees on top of those of underlying managers.

The principal case made against private equity these days is not so much that significant gains won't be made by investors in the asset – evidence for most of recent history supports private equity – rather it is that there is too much capital chasing too few deals and that, as a result, private equity funds won't be able to deploy their capital as fast as they might wish. The 2005 PriceWaterhouse/VentureEconomics report on private equity suggests that there may have been as much as $237 billion 'overhang' in private equity globally.[20]

In a 2004 report by Venture One it was noted that the venture funds alone had a capital overhang of $68 billion, with 25 per cent of funds raised in 2000, 54 per cent in 2001, 64 per cent in 2002 and 83 per cent in 2003, remaining unspent.[21]

Take-Away Advice

Fashions don't always make for good returns

The private equity industry is in vogue right now and a colossal volume of investor cash is being directed towards the sector. Deals are huge but multiples are rising with some reports that the prices being paid are now 50 per cent up on what they were five years ago.[22]

Allocations to private equity should be long term and modest

Private equity is capable of the very best of returns – as evidenced by any amount of performance data over the past three decades. However it won't all be straightforward and you'll need to be prepared for a long wait. I'd argue that private equity should form about 5–10 per cent of your portfolio at most and that you should be looking for areas of the market that aren't sporting too weighty a capital overhang.

Be prepared for capital calls and j-curves

Most private investors find private equity an odd sort of asset class, with 'capital committal periods' stretching for years despite it taking more time to see positive gains, even if they turn out to be spectacular.

The public–private trade-off is at hand

There is value to be had in the public equity market relative to most other asset classes. If portfolio managers in institutions don't bid up public equity valuations my bet is that the private equity firms will. Taking larger public firms back from the public markets may provide the deal flow that the private equity funds need.

2.8. Commodities – The Building Blocks of New Economies

The Futures Market for Commodities

Futures markets began as a kind of insurance, primarily for farmers and commodity producers. While their origins can be traced back to the Roman/Greek classical times the modern markets found their first standardisation in Chicago in 1848 with the first organised exchange. This market began in the mid-nineteenth century to provide a form of insurance against adverse market conditions. The 'futures' market, as it became known, was based in Chicago and because of that city's historical links to the beef and pork industry, the term 'pork belly' became the bellwether for the market. So, while Wall Street had the Dow Jones Index as its judge and jury for each day, LaSalle Street (where the big Chicago exchange is located) had the pork belly futures contract.

As it developed as a market, it attracted investors, speculators as well as those who needed it for hedging purposes. It also widened its scope to include financial instruments such as currencies, stock market indices and financial derivatives. Amongst the more recent (by which I mean in the last two decades) markets to explode in scale has been the options market.

A Small Part in History

Historically, direct investment in commodities has formed a relatively small part of the private investor's portfolio. Some investors historically endeavoured to get some form of exposure in their portfolios through indirect investment via either equities or bonds linked to business involved in the commodities sector such as gold mining or oil refinery. The experience has generally been one more correlated to the equity market than to the fortunes of the commodity market. In more recent times, however, investors have been able to get access more readily to the true economic exposure via futures, options and, even more recently, investable indices such as the Goldman Sachs Commodity Index, the S&P Commodity Index, or Dow Jones AIG Commodity Index. Most researchers agree that the use of such investments in the context of a wide portfolio can make excellent sense and offer diversification benefits to the conventional equity/bond/alternatives mix. Some evidence argues that the best diversification effects are to be had in periods of higher inflation such as was seen in the 1970s and 1980s when commodity prices soared and equities and bonds suffered. Research in this area also suggests that it is in bouts of unexpected inflation that commodities tend to perform strongest when compared to other asset classes.

Table 2.9 lists the performance characteristics of two of the major commodity indices. In isolation these sorts of returns and this sort of volatility should send any sensible investor running for the exits. It simply does not look very attractive as an investment class, suggesting that it takes a lot of skill to make substantial gains from direct commodity investment (perhaps less so in the commodities bull market of 2002–2005!)

Commodity trading advisors (CTAs), otherwise known as managed futures funds, are specialist hedge funds that invest in commodities usually via the futures markets. As a type of investment they are among the best diversifiers to include in a portfolio as they tend to be highly uncorrelated to equities, bonds and other types of hedge fund.

Commodities and Inflation

As a general rule, financial assets don't like inflation and real assets perform better in inflationary periods. Unexpected inflation – in other words inflation that financial markets have not factored in – can be particularly unwelcome, as interest rate responses impact on bond markets and in some instances on equity markets. As a general rule commodities usually do well in inflationary periods. This is almost self-evident in that, in many cases, commodities will be one of the first areas to be affected by the causes of inflation, be that demand-led or monetary in cause. As demand for goods

Table 2.9: Commodity Performance 1995–2005

Index	GS CSI	DJ/AIG CI
Annualised Return	10.5%	9.25%
Annualised Standard Deviation	20.65%	13.38%
Sharpe Ratio[*]	0.32	0.40
Maximum drawdown	−48.25%	−36.2%

* The Sharpe Ratio is a measure of risk adjusted return. It measures that level of return achieved over fixed interest returns, expressed as a percentage of the volatility of the investment.
Source: 'The Benefits of Commodity Investment' (2006), Center for International Securities and Derivatives Markets, Isenberg School of Management, University of Massachusetts.

2.8. Commodities – The Building Blocks of New Economies

and services rises, the price of those goods and services usually rises as well, which in turn can lead to rises in the price of the commodities needed to make those goods and services – hence why many argue that commodities are a natural hedge against inflation, even more so than property or equities. By contrast they tend not to do so well in periods of disinflation.

Commodities went through highs and lows in the 1980s and 1990s, but ended the two decade period of disinflation period at roughly the same level as they started. Behind this period of stagnation was lower investor demand for commodities as a hedge against inflation, and a shift in consumer spending to areas that were less commodity intensive.

Recent performance of commodity markets, in particular oil, has attracted a lot more attention than has been seen for many years.

In early November of 2004, oil prices had doubled when compared to the start of the year. By mid-2006, we had seen it double again, nearing $80, before falling back and beginning a downward trend in mid–late 2006.

While it hit headlines to a greater extent than other commodities – primarily because of its direct impact on the consumer – many other commodities, particularly metals, had also gone through dramatic price rises by 2006. Gold, from a five year low in 2001, had added over 50 per cent. Silver, from its low at the start of 2002, had added roughly 60 per cent. Copper, important to so much of the electronics industry, has more than doubled since mid-2002. However, it's never a uniform story in this part of markets, as other commodities have fallen in price (wheat by 30 per cent during 2004, corn by more than 40 per cent).

As can be seen in Figure 2.16, investors in commodity markets have done well in recent times and have seen gains outstrip the normally much less rewarding levels that the broad commodity market has generated. Oil has obviously played a huge role in this. Returns in 2006 were much less rewarding and it seems plausible that we are seeing a cyclical peak in this otherwise secular trend.

'Chindia' Will be the Engine for Commodities

One of the major sources of this general rise in commodity prices is a dramatic increase in the demand for commodities from the growing Chinese, Indian and other Asian economies, which is arguably a structural change in the global economy as opposed to a shorter-term change in demand.

Figure 2.16: 5 Year Rates of Returns from Commodities 1973–2006

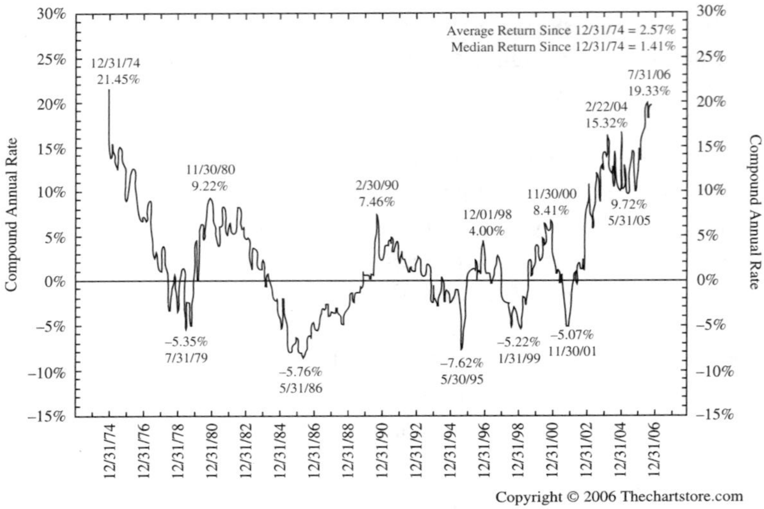

Source: <http://www.thechartstore.com>

If one assumes that global economic growth is set to continue, thereby increasing the demand for goods and services and the raw materials (i.e., commodities) used to manufacture them, the price of commodities – at least those with a finite supply – should offer opportunities to investors.

As the combined impact of China's and India's export economies pumps low-cost labour into the world economy, this should create a deflationary effect. However the demand that both create for commodities will engender an *inflationary* impact on commodity prices as it expands its manufacturing capacity. The story won't end there as, if successful at exporting their cheap labour advantage, the standard of living in both countries will rise. This will, as a consequence, further increase demand for commodities as both begin to generate middle-class demand on a massive scale.

In addition to the Chindia demand impact on commodity prices there are supply factors which also support the idea that commodities present a valuable opportunity for investors.

Most importantly commodity industries have been underinvested in for the past two decades when compared to higher returning manufacturing industry. Because of the typically long lead times to find sources and then build productive capacity, it is possible that production of commodities might not keep up with the growth in global demand.

Take-Away Advice

If you believe that the global economy is growing and that a large part of the growth will come from the emerging markets, then you cannot ignore commodity investing in the long run.

The term commodities, much like a lot of the broadly described asset classes, disguises a multitude. The indices that we've looked at here are to a degree dominated by the energies – especially oil. There is much more to commodity markets and it presents plenty of other money making opportunities.

At present I'd bet on the commodity market but I'd want to be able to take long and short positions and it's not a one way bet. Most commodities, with the exception of oil, are essentially limitless in their capacity, so it's far from sure that they'll go up in price.

Compared to bonds in your portfolio I suspect that commodities may have a more powerful engine behind them (demographics) in the coming decade.

In common with private equity, commodities present substantial risks to your capital and shouldn't form a large portion of your portfolio. In contrast to private equity however, liquidity is not a constraint.

2.9. Hedge Funds – The New Kid in Town

Introduction

The term 'hedge fund' straddles a wide variety of specialised investment strategies and techniques. Yet, probably the most defining characteristic of the hedge fund historically has been the fact that it has been almost the sole preserve of institutional investors and the very wealthiest private investors. Estimates vary widely but there are comfortably in excess of 7,500 of these funds around the globe managing close on a half a trillion dollars in wealth. The vast majority cannot be accessed by the 'ordinary' investor.

What has made them so attractive is the seeming ability of hedge funds to defy financial gravity when other assets are suffering losses. It is this 'low correlation' to other assets that make hedge funds so potentially useful to a portfolio. Equally the hedge fund industry does include some of the very best and brightest that the financial industry has to offer, so some funds can go a long way to making a person very wealthy indeed. It is not surprising that hedge funds began to thrive at a time when equity markets had seen some of their most dramatic losses in a generation.

Background and History

The term 'hedge fund' often means just that: 'hedging' is a term used to describe the protection of an asset or portfolio from adverse price changes. Despite its glamorous, even swashbuckling popular image, hedge funds are, at their heart, defensively oriented strategies with the most common types quite literally entailing each-way bets. The first hedge fund (see below) was established in 1949 although the industry has seen its most spectacular growth in the past decade, with most of the growth concentrated in the past five years.

Within the hedge funds industry, estimates of the pace of growth of funds under management form an almost ubiquitous part of every hedge fund manager's sales pitch. The jury may be out as the industry debates the effects of the mainstreaming of hedge fund techniques but their influence, or at least the influence of the investing techniques, is significant and likely to be lasting.

Primitive Origins

As with most sophisticated financial transaction techniques, if one scratches hard enough there are simple origins. 'Hedging' at the outset was a valuable business tool for farmers and producers of perishable goods whose income was made unpredictable by weather, market demands, tastes and conflict. By the early twentieth century, contracts had been created that could reduce the risk of adverse changes in weather patterns and market prices. These contracts, which permit the exchange of a specified quantity of an asset of a particular grade or quality at a specified price and time in the future, are aptly named 'futures'. While protecting themselves against future price declines, they forfeit the right to additional profits if prices rise. Likewise, users of these products often use futures contracts to hedge against future price increases, but they forfeit the benefits of future price declines.

Standardisation of futures contracts on exchanges made them easily transferable, inviting speculators into the futures markets. The vampires of the financial system? I disagree. Speculators are a critical part of the financial system since they take on price risk that the hedgers don't want, and they provide tremendous liquidity, making the exchange markets more efficient.

Thus markets emerged that include investors, hedgers, speculators and ultimately, arbitrageurs. These last participants act to ensure markets are efficiently priced and make their money by exploiting price anomalies.

Alfred Jones

No discussion of the role of hedge funds in the financial system could be complete without reference to Alfred Jones, the first hedge fund manager on Wall Street.

An associate editor at *Fortune* in the mid-1940s, Jones was working freelance by 1948, researching material for an article on forecasting trends in the market. The experts he interviewed at that time were unanimous about one thing – it was impossible to forecast the direction of the market. By the time he published an article in the March 1949 issue of *Fortune*,[23] he was already building an investment partnership to exploit what he felt he had discovered. (The article itself did little to reveal his techniques. It wasn't for another seventeen years before *Fortune* again covered what he was up to.), Alfred Jones's objective was to protect the value of his portfolio from falling market prices while identifying individual investments that would outperform in the short to medium term. Sounds like a strategy aiming at winning in rising and falling markets – a neat trick if it could be achieved. The method he would use was to buy ('go "long" equities') he felt were undervalued and 'go "short" equities' he felt were overvalued.

Short selling is a technique that is mostly associated with hedge fund strategies. Take an example of a stock that I believe will fall in value – ABC Limited, currently priced at $10. To gain from this fall, my first step is to borrow the share from someone else and sell the share, pocketing $10. When it comes to give back the share to the person from whom I borrowed it I will stand to gain, if indeed the share has fallen in value. For instance if it fell to $8, I could simply buy the share in the market at $8 and give it back to the stock lender – a roundtrip profit of $2.

Jones defined three principles of hedge funds as:

- you had to be short all the time – in other words something would always be falling in value;
- you always use leverage – the bank's capital can be very efficiently deployed;
- the manager receives 20 per cent of the profits – reward investment management the same way investors get rewarded.

Jones's model performed better than the US domestic equity market during the 1950s and, while it was unique, it remained at the periphery of Wall Street and the idea did not catch on until the 1960s. Indeed in 1966, *Fortune* published an article entitled 'The Jones nobody can keep up with', recognising his out-performance of the nearest mutual fund (Fidelity Trend Fund) by some 44 per cent over the previous five years and 87 per cent over the previous ten years (Dreyfus Fund). Imitators arrived on the scene in their hundreds quickly afterwards, before the environment of the early 1970s proved too savage for the less talented. So-called hedge strategies employed by the new managers were revealed as nothing more than leveraged equity funds. After the oil crises, most hedge funds disappeared or slumbered in obscurity.

In the decade following the 1974 market bottom, hedge funds returned to operating in relative obscurity, as they had prior to April 1966. During this period, comparatively few hedge funds were established, but among them was one of the best.

In May of 1986, 'The Red-Hot World of Julian Robertson' was explored in a cover feature of *Institutional Investor* – a US financial journal.[24] This cover story reported that Robertson's Tiger Fund had been compounding at 43 per cent during its first six years, net of expenses and incentive fees, versus 18.7 per cent for the S&P 500 index.

Once again, the hedge fund industry came into the spotlight with names such as Julian Robertson, Michael Steinhardt and George Soros foremost amongst the players in the market. The range and variety of hedge fund strategies grew during the 1980s as investment bankers and traders who believed they possessed a particular skill in exploiting pricing anomalies or

2.9. Hedge Funds – The New Kid in Town

profiting in declining markets left the security of their bank trading rooms to set up investment partnerships. These now include sector equity funds (biotechnology, telecommunications etc), dedicated short funds (funds that profit in declining markets), convertible bond and merger arbitrage funds, fixed income arbitrage and other relative value trading funds, technical trading funds, distressed securities funds, global macro-funds, developed market foreign funds, emerging market funds, a variety of market-neutral funds, a variety of derivatives-based funds and more. In addition, there are various types of 'fund of funds', which seek to diversify among different managers.

The continued growth of hedge funds in the 1990s forced the introduction of regulations, which served to ensure that the high standards of disclosure and accountability would begin to be enforced on hedge funds. However tight regulation and disclosure make uncomfortable bedfellows for individuals who believe, rightly or wrongly, that they have an unique insight into the market and who see their secret techniques as the basis of their being in business. Many funds established their operations offshore to avoid withholding taxes and to ensure that their investment strategies remained concealed from the eyes of the regulatory authorities. Hence the increasing popularity of locations such as Cayman Islands, British Virgin Islands and others for hedge fund domicile.

So What Makes a Hedge Fund Different Nowadays?

Today's version of a hedge fund continues to differ significantly from its traditional investment fund cousin in five ways:

- They have the ability to 'short' an asset.
- They leverage (borrow additional capital) to enhance potential performance.
- They are absolute return seekers, i.e. they strive to generate profits irrespective of the direction of the overall markets.
- The partners typically invest a substantial portion of their own capital alongside client assets.
- The partners are incentivised to perform through performance related fees.

Having a goal to realise profits in a variety of market conditions and not only in a rising stock market, makes a compelling sales story. Being less restricted in the techniques they can employ to reach their investment objectives, makes the story all the more plausible.

Growth of the Hedge Fund Industry

TASS Investment Research, which tracks the hedge fund industry, has calculated that hedge fund assets under management have grown by an average of 26 per cent per annum over the last six years. While estimates vary, there are believed to be about 7,500 hedge funds in existence by the start of 2007, managing roughly $1.4 trillion in assets. In the past couple of years, an increasing number of conservative investors such as pension funds, endowments and foundations have begun to allocate a substantial amount of assets to hedge funds. Figure 2.17 below demonstrates the extent of the growth in hedge funds since 1988 and serves to illustrate the growing importance of the sector to the wider financial system.

The vast majority of funds are relatively small when compared to traditional unit trusts and mutual funds, with funds under management of $100m or less. A review of the major databases suggests that only 50 per cent of hedge funds have assets exceeding $25m. In addition, less than 15 per cent of funds appear to have track records of ten years or more.

Figure 2.17: Estimated Global Hedge Fund Assets under Management

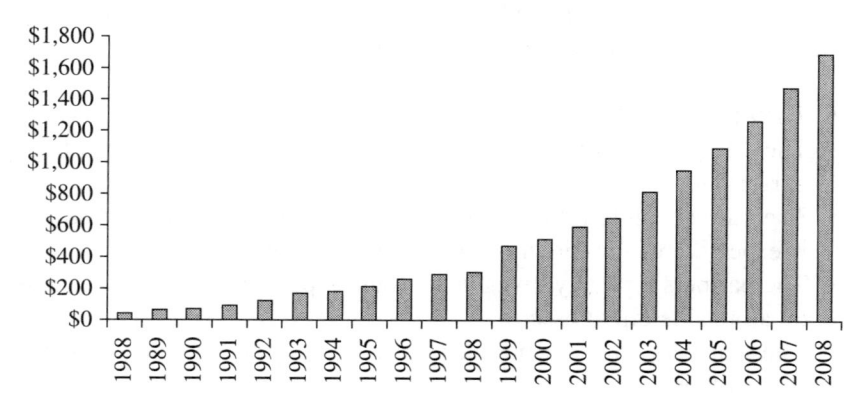

Note: Estimates for 2004–2008 are projections based on current data and may be revised in the future.
Source: Greenwich Alternative Investments LLC <http://greenwichai.com>.

2.9. Hedge Funds – The New Kid in Town

The industry still pales in comparison to the size of the mutual fund industry. The Investment Company Institute, the mutual fund industry association in the US, estimates that the size of the US assets in mutual funds is $7.2tn. We can reasonably assume that hedge fund assets represent less than 5 per cent of overall world mutual fund assets. However it is most probable that the techniques and methods used by hedge funds will become increasingly mainstream in the years to come.

The Main Types of Hedge Fund

Long/Short Equity

This strategy is the oldest and perhaps most readily comprehended and represents the fastest growing sector of the hedge fund world. Some estimates are that up to one-third of all hedge funds fall into this category. Typically a fund of this kind will invest in stocks that they believe will outperform in a given time period and will simultaneously 'short' those companies it believes are overvalued. The extent that a fund is either long or short is called the fund's 'net exposure' and most long/short equity managers are 'net long'.

Long/short equity funds will come in a number of specialist flavours, some specialising by sector or region, some by style, others focus on small caps. The vast majority of these funds operate in the mature liquid markets of the United States while a growing number are now trading European and Asian equities. The range of leverage employed varies from none (up to 100 per cent invested) to three times, although aggressive funds have been known to use larger amounts.

Equity Market-Neutral

A closely related variation of the long/short equity manager is found in the equity neutral style. What sets market-neutral firms apart is the manner in which they seek to fashion their portfolios in a way that hedges out all market-related risk. In crude terms, the long bets equal the short bets in quantum. More specifically, market neutral managers will often utilise complex mathematical models to determine the types of strategies required to remove the effect of market movements on the returns of their funds. With market neutrality achieved, these types of advisors will typically leverage the return on the portfolio through borrowing additional capital.

Equity Arbitrage

The equity arbitrageur buys or sells a basket of stocks and hedges with a future. What these managers are hoping to find is a change in expectations of the futures market that provides value opportunities when compared to the cash market. Typically these funds produce moderate returns with a little more volatility than is common to other arbitrage strategies.

Convertible Arbitrage

A convertible bond is a security issued by a company that offers the holder a fixed annual coupon payment, including face value at maturity as well as the right to convert the bond to a specified number of the company's ordinary shares at a specified price sometime in the future.

Convertible bonds demonstrate characteristics of both debt and equity and as a consequence an opportunity arises for knowledgeable traders to identify and exploit arbitrage opportunities. This will nearly always involve purchasing the bond and hedging it by shorting the stock into which it can be later converted. The extent to which the bond is hedged, as well as the degree of leverage employed, will vary from fund to fund.

Convertible bonds by their very nature have an attractive pay-off profile. During bearish conditions when the stock price falls, the fixed coupon continues to pay interest to the holder while the holder can participate in capital growth when the company performs favourably, eventually providing the opportunity to own the stock outright. In the event that a company defaults (or is downgraded by a rating agency) on its debt payments, the investor in a convertible arbitrage fund is protected as the manager will be short the stock of that company.

As a group, convertible bond funds tend to be lower risk and lower return than most other hedge fund styles.

Global Macro

The Global Macro funds essentially created the gun-slinging reputation of the hedge fund industry. Made famous by the George Soros's Quantum

2.9. Hedge Funds – The New Kid in Town

Fund in the early 1990s when the fund 'broke the Bank of England' through 'leveraged' bets on the anticipated movement in the value of Sterling.

Global Macro make bets on the trading opportunities in the global currency, interest rate and commodity sectors. Borrowing and trend-following are the principal characteristics as too is the more speculative nature of the strategies deployed by such funds. The speculative nature of Global Macro funds means that the volatility of returns tends to be greater than that exhibited by other types of hedge funds.

Fixed Income Arbitrage

This strategy involves searching for opportunities in the publicly-traded debt markets and exploiting pricing discrepancies between related securities.

A fixed income arbitrage manager will typically trade in and out of the largest and most traded debt, while simultaneously shorting a security from the same issuer. This typically involves neutralising the sensitivity of the portfolio to changes in market interest rates while capturing profitable event-driven or pricing discrepancies (due to credit considerations, for instance).

These strategies are endeavouring to find tiny pricing anomalies and leverage them massively to generate returns. Obviously such leverage is also a source of significant risk. Fixed income arbitrage strategies include yield curve arbitrage, credit spread arbitrage, mortgaged backed arbitrage and cash versus futures arbitrage.

Capitalism's four letter word...LTCM

Speak it in hushed tones: Long Term Capital Management (LTCM). Once described by Kevin Muehring in *Institutional Investor* as 'in effect the best finance faculty in the world',[25] LTCM included Nobel prize-winning economics professors amongst its advisors. However despite its illustrious intellectual staffing, in the late 1990s as Brazil, Indonesia and Russia's markets all crashed within months of each other, LTCM, which was a fixed income arbitrageur of kinds, came crashing down and almost brought the banking system with it. While the majority of fixed income arbitrage traders employ gearing in the range of three to five times, LTCM at one stage used its $2.2bn of equity to buy securities worth $125bn. Ultimately, its trades led to trillions of dollars of exposure within the financial system. As key relationships between markets (which formed the basic tenets of their risk management systems) broke down, the fund became dangerously exposed. It soon became apparent that the derivative positions used to shield the fund from losses were actually adding considerably to them. It took the combined will of all the major investment banks to bail out what was left of LTCM to protect the banking system itself.

Merger Arbitrage

The job of a merger arbitrageur (also known as risk arbitrageur) is to profit from the share-price movements that arise as a consequence of a planned merger. Most typically merger arbitrage funds generate returns by purchasing the stock of the company being acquired (long position) and shorting the stock of the acquiring company.

When a company announces its plans to take over another company the acquirer will usually offer a purchase price that is at a premium to the current stock market value. If it's $10 in the market today they may offer $11 to secure enough shares to effect the takeover. The merger arbitrageur makes a judgement call as to whether the takeover will occur at this price. As the acquiring company's shares may decline if the market perceives that the company has to borrow too much to finance the purchase, an arbitrage opportunity can arise, resulting in a profit from the rising stock price of the acquired and the declining stock price of the acquirer. Success tends to depend on whether such deals are completed or not.

As a style these funds fared well when there was a supply of corporate activity.

Distressed Debt/High-Yield Investing

Distressed-debt managers buy into the equity or debt of companies in financial distress who may not have the resources to repay interest or principal to its lenders. The success of these funds depends on the research ability of the manager to find opportunities and participate in a sector of the market that is tainted by failure, in the expectation that extraordinary profits will be earned. Unsurprisingly, such funds do well in periods of strong economic growth.

2.9. Hedge Funds – The New Kid in Town

Managed Futures

One of the largest groupings of hedge fund/alternative investment styles are the so called 'managed futures' or 'commodity trading advisors', large and distinct enough to be considered in isolation from other alternative managers. By Q4 2006, it was estimated that $170bn was under management by CTAs, up from about $10bn in 1990.[26]

In common with hedge fund managers, CTAs employ leverage, invest both long and short, have fee arrangements involving both performance and management fees and tend to operate from more lightly regulated jurisdictions. They principally invest in physical commodities, futures and options. CTAs provide managed accounts to investors whereas their near cousin CPOs, or commodity pool operators, provide pooled funds. To complicate matters, many hedge funds register as CPOs. There are significant differences particularly when it comes to the nature of leverage deployed, tax reporting and use of derivatives, but to the naked eye the differences appear subtle!

Short Selling

If long-only investing is what you are accustomed to as an investor – buying an asset in order to profit from a growth in its price – then short selling is the antithesis of this: a method of investing that profits from a fall in the price of an asset.

To bring about a 'short sale' the fund borrows the target security from a third party and sells them in the market, pocketing what it sees as a 'high price'. Presuming the fund is correct, after the stock price has declined the fund buys the stock back cheaply and returns the stock to the owner, retaining the difference in price as profit. However, if the price of the stock rises during this transaction, the trade will result in losses for the short seller.

Historical Performance of Hedge Funds: Risk and Return in the Hedge Fund World

A snapshot of the past decade or so suggests that hedge funds have, at minimum, kept pace with equities over the long run and have done so in a steadier fashion without suffering losses of a comparable magnitude *en route*.

Of course the term 'hedge fund' disguises a multitude with the various differing styles of hedge fund showing markedly different patterns of performance.

Before proceeding, a word about such hedge fund performance figures. They are the subject of much academic debate as to their reliability, primarily because of 'survivorship bias' – their tendency not to report as many of the failed hedge funds as might be appropriate. Some commentators have been very critical in their analysis, suggesting that the performance claimed for hedge funds in published indices are inflated by a number of percentage points. Suffice to say, some caution is merited.

Table 2.10 lists the performances of some of the major hedge fund styles over the past decade. As you can see, the 'average' of hedge funds disguises a multitude of varying performances.

Adding a great deal of leverage, short selling and derivatives and you'd imagine the cost is much, much more risk. However, what tends to be the case is that, in the aggregate, there are much more controlled, balanced performances than are seen in traditional long-only investing. While most live up to this literal interpretation by producing 'hedged' returns, there are nonetheless hedge fund strategies that live up to the gun-slinging reputation.

By calculating the risk incurred in earning these returns we can evaluate if the strategies provide sufficient return to the investor for the risk undertaken. Table 2.11 introduces some of the risk measures that can be used to evaluate the level of risks taken by each of the strategy types.

Two of the measures that you may find unfamiliar are 'Beta' and the 'Sharpe Ratio'. 'Beta' is basically a measure of the sensitivity of the strategy to the market in general. A high beta usually indicates a riskier strategy. The Sharpe Ratio measures the return achieved per unit of risk taken. When looked at together a magician investor might achieve a high Sharpe with a low beta. Take care on reading too much into these measures, however. They are two among many such measures and all have their flaws. They are about as useful as a GP taking your temperature and your blood pressure – it will help to make a diagnosis but you'd be disappointed if that was all the examination you got for your €50!

A Word about 'Fund of Funds'

By now it should be apparent that this is a complex field, and one filled with its fair share of both genius and charlatanism. A useful expert

Table 2.10: Historical Annual Returns for Hedge Fund Styles (1994-2006)

	1994	1995	1996	1997	1998	1999	2000	2001	2002	2003	2004	2005	2006
Hedge Funds	-4.35	21.68	22.22	25.94	-0.36	23.43	4.85	4.42	3.04	15.44	9.64	7.61	6.1
L/S Equity	-8.10	23.03	17.14	21.46	17.19	47.22	2.66	-3.65	-1.6	17.27	11.56	9.68	5.2
Equity Market Neutral	-2.00	11.04	16.60	14.83	13.31	15.33	14.99	9.31	7.42	7.07	6.48	6.14	6.8
Convertible Arbitrage	-8.06	16.55	17.87	14.48	-4.42	16.04	25.64	14.58	4.05	12.9	1.98	-2.55	7.48
Global Macro	-5.72	30.67	25.58	37.11	-3.64	5.81	11.67	18.38	14.66	17.99	8.49	9.25	8.6
Fixed Income Arbitrage	0.31	12.50	15.93	9.34	-8.16	12.11	6.29	8.04	5.75	7.97	6.86	0.63	5.65
Event Driven	0.75	18.34	23.06	19.96	-4.87	22.26	7.26	11.5	0.16	20.02	14.47	8.95	7.35
Managed Futures	11.95	-7.10	11.97	3.12	20.64	-4.69	4.24	1.9	18.33	14.13	5.97	-0.11	2.13
Short Selling	14.91	-7.35	-5.48	0.42	-6.00	-14.22	15.76	-3.58	18.14	-32.59	-7.72	17.0	3.58

Source: Data from Credit Suisse Tremont Index LLC, 'Returns for 2006 to end June', <http://www.hedgeindex.com/hedgeindex/en/default.aspx?cy = USD>, accessed 9/11/2006. Copyright © 2006, Credit Suisse/Tremont Index LLC. All rights reserved. Tables 2.10 and 2.11 (the "Work") are provided by the author Kevin Quinn, who takes full responsibility for providing these. Neither Credit Suisse/Tremont Index LLC nor its affiliates, subsidiaries, members or parents (collectively, "Credit Suisse") have undertaken any review of this Work or any recommendations contained herein, or of the suitability of this information for anyone accessing this Work, and neither the Work nor the information contained in the Work is sponsored, endorsed or approved by Credit Suisse. The Credit Suisse/Tremont Hedge Fund Index, the Credit Suisse/Tremont Investable Hedge Fund Index, and the corresponding Sub-Indices, and any information in the Work relating thereto (collectively, the "Information") is made available to you for your own internal use and may not be reproduced or disseminated in any form, nor may it be used to create, offer or sell any security, financial instrument or index. The Information is provided "as is" and any use is at your entire risk. CREDIT SUISSE DISCLAIMS ANY AND ALL REPRESENTATIONS AND WARRANTIES, WHETHER EXPRESS, IMPLIED OR STATUTORY, REGARDING THE INFORMATION, INCLUDING WITHOUT LIMITATION, ANY WARRANTY REGARDING MERCHANTABILITY, FITNESS FOR A PARTICULAR PURPOSE, QUALITY, OR NON-INFRINGEMENT, AND ANY WARRANTY REGARDING THE ACCURACY, TIMELINESS, SUITABILITY, AVAILABILITY OR COMPLETENESS OF THE INFORMATION, OR THE RESULTS OBTAINED FROM THE USE THEREOF. UNDER NO CIRCUMSTANCES AND UNDER NO THEORY OF LAW, TORT, CONTRACT, STRICT LIABILITY OR OTHERWISE, WILL CREDIT SUISSE HAVE ANY LIABILITY IN CONNECTION WITH THE INFORMATION OR THE USE THEREOF OR THE RESULTS OBTAINED FROM SUCH USE, WHETHER DIRECT OR INDIRECT, INCLUDING SPECIAL, INCIDENTAL, CONSEQUENTIAL, EXEMPLARY OR PUNITIVE DAMAGES, AND INCLUDING, WITHOUT LIMITATION, ANY DAMAGES BASED ON LOSS OF PROFITS, LOSS OF USE, BUSINESS INTERRUPTION OR LOSS OF DATA, EVEN IF CREDIT SUISSE HAS BEEN ADVISED OF THE POSSIBILITY OF SUCH DAMAGES OR WAS NEGLIGENT.

Table 2.11: Historical Risk, Return and Value Added (1994–2004)

Index	Average Month	Best Month	Worst Month	Beta	Sharpe
CSFB/Tremont Hedge Fund Index	0.88%	8.53%	−7.55%	0.26	0.82
Convertible Arbitrage	0.8%	3.57%	−4.68%	0.04	1.26
Dedicated Short	−0.07%	22.71%	−8.69%	−0.87	−0.35
Emerging Markets	0.68%	16.42%	−23.03%	0.54	0.17
Equity Mkt Neutral	0.82%	3.26%	−1.15%	0.08	2.09
Event Driven	0.91%	3.68%	−11.77%	0.21	1.24
Distressed	1.06%	4.1%	−12.45%	0.23	1.37
E.D. Multi-Strategy	0.83%	4.66%	−11.52%	0.19	1.00
Risk Arbitrage	0.65%	3.81%	−6.15%	0.13	0.92
Fixed Income Arb	0.57%	2.02%	−6.96%	0.01	0.77
Global Macro	1.17%	10.6%	−11.55%	0.19	0.87
Long/Short Equity	0.97%	13.01%	−11.43%	0.42	0.71
Managed Futures	0.56%	9.95%	−9.35%	−0.16	0.18
Multi-Strategy	0.76%	3.61%	−4.76%	0.02	1.22
MSCI World	0.67%	9.06%	−13.32%	0.86	0.22
S&P 500	0.93%	9.67%	−14.46%	1	0.42

Source: Credit Suisse First Tremont LLC (2004). Compiled from data on <http://www.hedgeindex.com>. Copyright © 2006, Credit Suisse/Tremont Index LLC. All rights reserved. See under Table 2.10 on page 99 for further details.

intermediary in the field is the 'fund of funds', companies that specialise in combining the various specialisms into diversified pooled funds.

For investors who do not have the time to devote to due diligence in each specialism, fund of funds can provide a useful conduit to gain exposure to hedge funds as part of a portfolio. Additionally some of the more established 'fund of funds' are well-connected to the world's best managers, managers that are typically no longer easily accessed.

The downside to fund of funds is that the fees charged are usually high. As well as paying a management and incentive fee to each of the underlying advisors, the fund of fund manager will charge a management fee of between 1.5 per cent and 2.5 per cent. A performance-related fee may also apply, typically between 10 per cent and 20 per cent of the profits of the fund of funds.

It is believed that fund of funds now control roughly one-quarter of the assets under management in the hedge fund industry. I believe that this will increase as these funds are likely to feature prominently in the future, both for institutional investors and for private investors, as will be the case with private equity fund of funds. However few, if any, will deliver spectacular performances. What's more probable is that fund of funds returns will be ahead of cash and provide very low volatility.

So How Much Should I Have?

The key questions investors should be asking when it comes to hedge funds are:

- What role can hedge funds play in a portfolio?
- How much allocation to hedge funds should I have?
- What type of hedge fund should I have?

Hedge funds remain a difficult to understand, lightly regulated, esoteric investment to most investors. Yet as a category they do have some exceptionally valuable characteristics. Firstly, when thought of as part of a wider portfolio, they can, in theory, add an unusually powerful amount of risk reduction. This is primarily because they appear to be less well correlated with the direction of equity and bond markets. In demonstrating this characteristic, there are of course periods where the rules get broken, such as in 2002 when many hedge funds performed very poorly along with the equity market. Most commentators argue now that there is a growing correlation between hedge fund performances and the broader equity market. Nonetheless the hedge fund techniques of shorting and leverage are likely to gain sway in more mainstream investing in years to come and will be part of many investors' portfolios in some shape.

The Effect of Adding Hedge Funds to Traditional Portfolios

Traditional-style portfolios of stocks and bonds may benefit significantly, both in returns and risks, from the addition of hedge funds. Figure 2.18 shows the result of adding, to a traditional 60/40 equity index/bond index portfolio, increasing amounts of each of the average hedge fund styles. As hedge funds are added, returns increase and risk (standard deviation) is held constant.

The hedge fund industry has of course been busy in recent years extolling the virtue of its low correlation to equities, most particularly as equities nose-dived. Figure 2.18 suggests that a traditional 60/40 equity/bond

Figure 2.18: The Effect of Adding Hedge Funds to a Traditional Portfolio

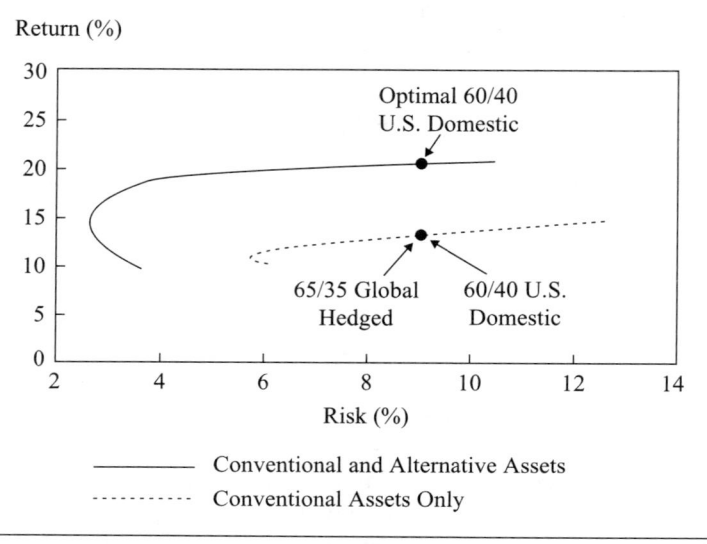

```
Return (%)
30 |
25 |              Optimal 60/40
                  U.S. Domestic
20 |                    ●
15 |
          _____●_____
10 |     /
        /      65/35 Global      60/40 U.S.
 5 |           Hedged            Domestic
 0 |____|____|____|____|____|____|____
    2    4    6    8   10   12   14
                 Risk (%)
```

——————— Conventional and Alternative Assets
- - - - - - - Conventional Assets Only

Note: Based on annual data for 1981–2000.
Source: B. Singer, R. Staub and K. Terhaar (2002), 'Determining Appropriate Allocations to Alternative Investments', *Financial Analysts Journal*, Vol. 2002, No. 2, pp. 4–15. Copyright © 2002, CFA Institute. Reproduced and republished from The Financial Analysts Journal with permission from CFA Institute. All rights reserved.

portfolio would have underperformed and been considerably more volatile than a portfolio that also included 35 per cent in hedge funds.

What is at the heart of this is the purportedly lower correlation of alternative assets to the principal assets. Table 2.12, drawn from Brinson Partners' 2002 paper[27] for AIMR (now CFA© Institute) serves to illustrate that hedge funds in general are indeed quite positively correlated to equities. Including hedge funds is not, therefore, some kind of free lunch. Indeed, in studies produced by Gaurav Amin and Harry Kat there is strong suggestion that introducing hedge funds into a portfolio, while capable of reducing variation as measured conventionally, might also increase the odds of an 'outlier' occurring.[28] In other words, in general hedge funds in your portfolio should help to reduce the ups and downs but once in a while they might do something spectacular or indeed something pretty awful.

Table 2.12: Traditional and Alternative Investments, Historical Return, Volatility, and Correlation Characteristics

Asset Class	1	2	3	4	5	6	7	8	Return	Volatility
1. U.S. equity	1.00								14.8%	12.8%
2. Non-U.S. equity	0.55	1.00							13.2	16.7
3. U.S. fixed income	0.35	0.14	1.00						10.5	7.0
4. Non-U.S. fixed income	0.24	0.29	0.73	1.00					10.7	6.0
5. Private equity	−0.46	0.00	−0.47	−0.10	1.00				20.7	10.5
6. Real estate	−0.01	0.39	−0.05	0.23	0.47	1.00			7.8	5.9
7. Natural resources	0.33	0.25	0.17	−0.08	−0.53	−0.51	1.00		18.3	8.8
8. Hedge funds	0.71	0.52	0.31	0.14	−0.30	−0.18	0.23	1.00	18.2	9.4

Note: Based on annual logarithmic excess return for 1981–2000 (national resources for 1987–2000).
Source: B. Singer, R. Staub and K. Terhaar (2002), 'Determining Appropriate Allocations to Alternative Investments', *Financial Analysts Journal*, Vol. 2002, No. 2, pp. 4–15. Copyright 2002, CFA Institute. All rights reserved. Copyright © 2002, CFA Institute. Reproduced and republished from The Financial Analysts Journal with permission from CFA Institute. All rights reserved.

In short, for the most part, it's a good thing to have in your portfolio, but it's far from a panacea for risk and may in extreme circumstances be very ineffective.

However, if one digs a level deeper and looks at some of the individual types of hedge funds, one gets a better appreciation. Once again treating hedge funds as a monolith is a flawed way of thinking. Instead one needs to look to the correlations on each style to appreciate that there are many that are indeed outstanding at reducing risk as they demonstrate very low, even negative correlations to the major assets. In 2004 Allison and Lin suggested that fixed income arbitrage, equity market-neutral and convertible bonds all have very little link to the performance of equity markets.[29] Merger arbitrage and distressed securities rest in the middle with long/short equity the most connected to the direction of equities.

Other Risks

Before deciding to include hedge funds in a portfolio, investors should also be aware of some of the other risks that go with alternative investing. Borrowing again from Allison and Lin there are a list of eight non-return-related areas that investors need to be conscious of:

Lower Level of Regulation

The lower level of level of regulation means greater risk of fraud or 'blow ups'. These risks are very real and investors are well advised to diversify into multiple hedge fund strategies.

Less or No Transparency

When compared to the traditional investments, hedge funds are pretty secretive. What this means is that there is a risk that cannot be seen in the numbers. How much leverage was used? Did they do what they said they'd do?

Tax Efficiency

Ireland is blessed with a very effective taxation of funds – one 'gross roll-up' rate applies to all unit funds and in many instances this can be applied to hedge funds licensed for business here. However, the vast majority of

2.9. Hedge Funds – The New Kid in Town

hedge funds are domiciled far beyond Ireland and, as such, are unlikely to be tax efficient. Classified as offshore funds, most hedge funds are likely to attract marginal rate tax on gains in the hands of Irish residents.

Lack of Liquidity

Lock up periods, limited accessibility and less frequent pricing all make the hedge fund investment, while more liquid than property, still a pretty clunky one, when compared to big, regularly priced securities markets.

Complexity of Strategies

Most people don't like investing in something they don't understand and when it comes to hedge fund strategies there is often plenty that is not understood by client and advisor alike. The result is a perception of risk that does not differentiate between what is truly risky and what is not.

Greater Firm-Specific (Business) Risk

Despite all the talk of risk management and diversification effects, you can lose all your money in a hedge fund. Principally this comes from the fact that so many hedge funds are 'one man and his dog' operations that can go bust.

Greater Fees

The fees for hedge funds are much greater than those for traditional funds and typically include a management fee of 1 to 1.5 per cent plus a performance fee amounting to 20 per cent of gains. Some have the manners to place the performance at gains over a certain target level but that doesn't detract from the fact that hedge funds are expensive. Some argue this is a virtue as it means managers simply manage money instead of chasing sales targets.

Potential for Leverage to Amplify Negative Returns

Leverage cuts both ways. In good times it serves to amplify returns. But in bad times it simply exacerbates losses. In dreadful times, it can leave investors owing money.

Wealth Management

> ### Take-Away Advice
>
> I believe that hedge funds have a big role to play in a market where asset returns are more muted than we've seen for a generation. However, I don't believe that the price one pays for hedge funds makes them particularly effective in their own right. They are better off used as part of a portfolio and used in a manner that serves to reduce the risk of the overall portfolio – as opposed to being a principal source of return. If you read enough of the recommendations from academics you'll find allocations ranging anywhere from 5 per cent to 25 per cent being justified. I believe that a meaningful level of risk reduction is achieved at about 12–15 per cent of a portfolio – any smaller and it becomes less meaningful, any greater and it becomes expensive and increases the risk of a blue-moon event damaging a portfolio, to which this form of investing is exposed.
>
> If you use a fund of hedge funds then expect returns to be more muted – roughly in line with the added cost involved – and consequently to be 'cash plus' in nature.

2.10. Asset Class Almanac 2007

Asset Class Performance in Perspective

From the perspective of the last two and half decades, there's one defining characteristic of a portfolio with all the major asset classes I've described in this section: none win all the time. In fact if anything this is the only 100 per cent guaranteed promise that can be made in any wealth management plan you might care to discuss.

What is noteworthy in Table 2.13 is that throughout the period 1978–2006, there was no single year where cash was truly king. Only when one removed the 'alternative' assets from the fray and placed cash against traditional 'long-only' assets would cash have come to the fore during difficult market conditions. The data for the alternative classes (private equity and hedge funds) must always be treated with a dose of scepticism. They are often criticised for presenting a rose-tinted version of performance. Nonetheless, in the aggregate, this information shows us the potential that exists beyond the conventional. For most table-topping performances one must look to public equity, hedge funds and private equity with, surprisingly,

Table 2.13: Asset Class Returns 1978–2006

	Inflation	Cash	Bonds	Property	Public Equity	Hedge Funds	Commodities
1978	7.9%	9.7%	−2.4%	26.3%	14.8%	18.6%	13.63%
1979	15.9%	14.4%	−0.6%	25.8%	8.6%	**30.96%**	23.68%
1980	18.2%	14.6%	12.6%	22.1%	**27.7%**	27.6%	9.59%
1981	23.3%	16.2%	2.1%	**17.8%**	3.6%	7.2%	−17.37%
1982	12.3%	13.4%	**44.6%**	9.0%	14.9%	25.2%	−8.2%
1983	10.3%	10.5%	11.9%	8.3%	**45.8%**	18.2%	18.63%
1984	6.7%	11.6%	11.1%	7.2%	12.0%	**15.7%**	−12.03%
1985	4.9%	10.6%	25.1%	6.4%	37.2%	32.0%	−6.07%
1986	3.2%	9.5%	13.8%	8.6%	32.4%	19.5%	−8.85%
1987	3.1%	8.4%	14.8%	14.6%	3.3%	15.24%	11.22%
1988	2.7%	9.0%	17.0%	19.0%	23.5%	**26.26%**	8.3%
1989	4.7%	11.9%	8.8%	19.5%	**32.7%**	30.37%	−8.7%
1990	2.7%	11.9%	4.6%	1.8%	−14.0%	14.76%	−3.17%
1991	3.6%	9.3%	15.0%	−2.8%	**23.4%**	31.8%	−6.54%
1992	2.3%	10.1%	9.9%	−2.7%	6.5%	18.5%	−2.56%
1993	1.5%	5.2%	28.7%	9.5%	**32.2%**	21.34%	11.61%
1994	2.4%	5.5%	−9.5%	11.3%	−1.2%	−4.35%	4.56%
1995	2.4%	6.1%	22.6%	8.1%	**28.5%**	21.68%	2.76%
1996	1.9%	5.9%	6.8%	13.1%	21.7%	**22.22%**	−1.47%
1997	1.9%	6.2%	18.3%	18.7%	**36.6%**	25.94%	−4.37%
1998	1.7%	5.6%	18.6%	22.0%	**22.6%**	−0.36%	−16.55%
1999	3.4%	4.7%	−6.3%	19.1%	15.7%	**23.43%**	7.28%
2000	5.9%	5.9%	13.8%	16.9%	0.2%	4.85%	11.06%
2001	4.2%	4.0%	3.4%	7.4%	−7.9%	4.42%	−16.34%
2002	5%	2.9%	12.9%	5.9%	−24.4%	3.04%	**23.04%**

(*Continued*)

Table 2.13 (*Cont'd*)

	Inflation	Cash	Bonds	Property	Public Equity	Hedge Funds	Commodities
2003	1.9%	2.3%	4.5%	12.7%	**30.9%**	15.44%	8.86%
2004	2.6%	2.6%	9.9%	11.5%	13.6%	9.6%	**33.1%**
2005	2.6%	3.2%	5.9%	24.3%	11.3%	7.6%	**27.9%**
2006	4.0%	4.8%	−5.0%	**27.2%**	7.4%	13.9%	−16.9%

Data sources:
1. Irish inflation as measured by the Central Statistics office.
2. Cash as measured by a combination of the US 3 month Treasury, the UK Interbank rate and the Irish Interbank rate to 2002; *Source*: Bank of Ireland Asset Management. For 2003–2005, the average of the 3 month US, UK and Euro yields are used. 2006 figure is the year end average of 3 month rates from each.
3. Bonds as measured by a combination of the Merrill Lynch 10 year Treasury Index, the UK JP Morgan Total Return Government Bond Index and the Riada/ABN 10 year Irish Bond Return. *Source*: Bank of Ireland Asset Management. 2006 figures from JP Morgan Global bond in euros (*source*: Moneymate).
4. Property is the total return of the Irish IPD Index.
5. Equities to 2002 as measured by the S&P 500 Total Return, the FTSE All Share Total Return and the ISEQ Total Return. *Source*: Bank of Ireland Asset Management. From 2004 equities represented by MSCI World Total Return Index in euros.
6. Hedge funds measured by the CSFB Tremont Hedge Fund Index 1994–2005 and by the Hennessee Hedge Index, 1988–1993. Performance 1978–1987 is drawn from a paper published by Harri and Brorsen 'Performance persistence and source of returns for hedge funds' July 2002. The data for this period covers a small sample of hedge funds and is therefore less representative than the more broadly based indices.
7. Commodities are represented by the CRB Index based on year end closing levels, expressed in dollars; 2004–2006 are expressed in euros.

property someway behind. What distinguishes property is the fact that it displays much more consistency in performance and more frequently claims the second place. Unlike many pursuits, being consistently second in the asset class performance tables is a very attractive place to be.

Because of the peculiarity of the cash flows associated with private equity, annual performance is less meaningful for direct comparison. However, if one were to include the private equity numbers and were to choose simply US numbers it would top the gold medal count. The same could be said for property were one to confine oneself to Ireland. Private equity gold medals would come to the fore if one focussed exclusively on the top quartile of private equity which would be some distance ahead of all-comers.

What this says to me is that there must be a role for almost every asset class in an investment portfolio. So all investors must somehow adopt a view on the roles and prospects of each. As you will have already seen there is a case to be made for and against each to varying degrees. The extent of performance from each asset class in 2007 and beyond is probably little more than crystal ball gazing, even if partially informed crystal ball gazing, but you may as well get your money's worth and I'll add my name to the list of failed forecasters! So here's my asset class almanac for 2007.

Interest Rates and Bonds

The US has been increasing rates at a predictable pace in recent times. At time of writing Bernanke had indicated that there may be a pause in US tightening, meaning we may be at the end of the interest rate cycle for now.

The EU began 2005 on the precipice of increasing rates, then thought the better of it and decided simply that rates wouldn't fall as economic stagnation in Germany and France required rates to be more subdued than anticipated. Towards the middle of the year stronger growth in the core EU economies might have given cause for an increase to come back on the radar as too did the stubbornly high level of oil prices. Monsieur Trichet changed his tone slightly towards the end of the year and the first of the rate changes appeared towards the year end. 2006 saw the start of the interest increases from the ECB as equivocation was sprinkled with modest increases. Expect more rate increases in the coming year. That will leave bonds markets as a somewhat less hospitable haven for the short term. The UK, which had lapsed into interest rate cuts, has renewed its regime of interest rate increases, although it is unlikely to be persistent.

Equities

Equities had a great run in 2005 and for a large part of 2006. Nonetheless we are now four years into a solid bull run in equities, with memories of the Great Bear Market behind us. Frustratingly it is probably accurate to say that equities are at fair value – neither too hot nor too cold and consequently, left to their own devices, might grind out solid enough returns in the coming year or two. We will need the tightening cycle (interest rate increases) to get behind us before we can get clear light on the direction for public equities. A combination of mid-teen multiples and falling rates of profit growth, may make stellar returns difficult to achieve. The dilemma is that the valuations levels are now at less challenging levels than they've been for the best part of fifteen years, yet corporate earnings are on the downward slope in growth terms. Only the Asian markets which come with a higher risk warning may again generate outsize returns. That's, however, looking at equities in isolation. What's harder to ignore is the fact that, on a relative valuation basis, equities are the cheapest of the main public asset classes. The momentum that might arise could drive equity returns much further north in the relatively short term. In early 2006, with most major public equity markets trading at forward P/Es of 13–14 times earnings, it seemed possible that another bumper crop was en route. Then a bout of self doubt hit markets in the middle of the year as interest increases hit home and continued geopolitical uncertainty in the Middle East left markets reeling. The latter part of 2006 saw solid recovery and the relative valuation of equities should make them more sought after from this juncture.

One anomaly that was apparent from the vantage point of early 2006 is the seemingly relentless out-performance of smaller companies over large blue chips. One can rationally expect this to be reversed at some point. This began to be in evidence in the middle of 2006 and one can expect this to be a theme that may play out over the coming 3–5 years.

Property

The Irish residential market is not offering investors much value – time to think of it as providing somewhere to live primarily. Though well supported by the strong demographics Ireland exhibits, the spate of failed auctions in mid 2006 served as a salutary reminder that prices can get away from even the most solid of investment classes.

2.10. Asset Class Almanac 2007

UK commercial property will continue to be the immediate beneficiary of Irish capital flows but it too will be far from a uniform story – sterling interest rates have risen and taken the shine off its residential market. Even a softening in UK monetary policy may not reignite this market. So where else? Other major Western economies continue to provide solid, if unspectacular, potential without the currency risk. The US commercial market looks a risky enough bet, primarily because of gains made in recent times and the sheer weight of capital it is attracting. For euro based investors it may be as much a currency play (with the attendant risks) as a property play. However, there are a lot of investors chasing the market and most are finding that they are in a long queue of buyers, which never augurs well for investment returns. Yield compression, and rising rates in most of the Western economies mean rental growth is the remaining growth ingredient. Nonetheless, it's time for greater caution in the conventional markets and time to be braver in more far flung places.

Hedge Funds, Commodities and Private Equity

In the wacky world of alternatives there are always spectacular gains to be made and huge losses waiting for the unwary. So I'm not going to predict it. However, what I will say is that a return of some degree of volatility will be necessary for hedge funds to make money in 2007 – they performed poorly in 2004 as most markets looked 'becalmed' and 2005 and 2006 were much the same. Expect some of the strategies – merger arbitrage, long-short equity and at some point distressed debt – to fare better.

As for private equity, invention, innovation and clever financial engineering will deliver, as ever. Proponents argue that it is a superior economic model. If one can find a top quartile fund, it's hard to argue with this. There is however an overhang of capital, meaning too many investors chasing too many deals and the valuations that are being paid for private equity deals have been exceeding public equity valuations in some instances, an anomaly that will not persist. Given the nature of private equity returns, it will be a long time before anyone knows for sure. Speculation is that private equity firms, as a result of the extent of cash at their disposal, will be very active in the years to come, so expect some big headlines.

Commodities may well continue their recent run, but bet on these as a secular (longer-term) trend. Interestingly, the spate of 'long-only' commodity products that became the vogue a year or two ago have disappeared to be replaced by 'long-short' commodity offerings; a clue that most pundits think things might be bumpier in the next few years. Nonetheless, as demand from the Far East really bites in the coming decade, be prepared for a cyclical turn in a lot of commodities. A must-have for your portfolio, but allow maximum flexibility.

With all its resources, the forecasting business means getting it wrong as often as getting it right. Individual year-on-year forecasts are simply unreliable. Instead, I would suggest that there are some much more reliable longer-term secular trends that can inform your decision making. These trends won't necessarily pay off over the short term (which you can define as anything ranging from three to ten years, depending on which trend you focus upon). However in the longer run, these trends are likely to contribute more to the successful management of your wealth than many others.

Interest Rates and Bonds

Globally, inflation is unlikely to be re-sparked at any time in the near future at the scale seen a generation ago. The dramatic increases in oil prices and commodity prices in the past couple of years have not generated global inflation on a scale anything like that of the 1970s. Even a return of interest rates to normal levels should not be a cause for great concern. That suggests it is unlikely that cash will be an attractive home for longer-term funds at any time in the near future and all that bonds can offer is to continue to provide some element of stability in your portfolio. Probably no more than 10–20 per cent of your portfolio should be held in bonds, both government, corporate and high yield. But be prepared to see this component drop from time to time – it's safer than shares but only just.

Credit spreads will widen as credit defaults normalise making corporate debt a riskier place to be. Interest rate increases in most major markets will reach a cyclical peak in the coming two years.

Emerging market demand will both stoke up inflation through increases in commodity prices and will export lots of deflation through cheaper consumer goods.

Equities

The long-term engine of growth might put in a couple of good years but it is probably unlikely to steam ahead for a prolonged period. It's the 'probably' that gets investors every time – a solid weighting to equities is essential if you are to catch the wave in equity returns whenever it does kick in. At least 40–50 per cent of your portfolio should be allocated to the equity market. Expect its relative cheapness to be a driver for the short term and its fair-priced nature to act as a brake in the medium term. Don't expect it to do much more than 7–9 per cent per annum over the long run. As for where, it's likely that Asia will come to the fore to a far greater extent in the years to come – the sheer scale of the emerging Chinese economy will rebalance global economic flows dramatically and equity markets won't ignore that.

In the shorter term expect markets to take some of the risk off the table as a rotation out of the riskier parts of the market sees the largely unrewarded bigger companies come back in favour.

Property

International property markets are attracting a colossal flow of capital at present, which is understandable given the performance of public equity markets. When returns are 'super-sized' as they have been in the global property market, the next phase is usually an oversupply of capital, which is where we are going. With long queues forming amongst institutional investors, 'yield compression' has been the order of the day. The yields in bond markets will act as a brake on how far property yields can compress and consequently it's reasonable to contend that this phase is behind us.

The Irish and UK residential and commercial markets have probably run out of steam somewhat. Major European and US markets both offer huge scope for investment – just don't expect the one-way trip that Ireland has afforded investors in the past decade. Some deals can boast IRRs in the 10 per cent plus category but they are fewer and thinner on the ground. My view is that about 20 per cent of an investor's equity should be in the property market, with the bulk of this in Western Europe, followed by lower allocation to the Far East (including allocations to emerging China and India) and the US. The risk is that a second bubble has emerged in Western property markets – much has been written of the price rises in countries such as Ireland, Britain, Australia, the US, The Netherlands and others. A lot of this is hyperbole, but any asset that has seen significant appreciation must, almost axiomatically, present greater risk. In property terms, don't ignore the Far East – the growth in these economies and the urbanisation that will be a theme for a generation will make for rich if volatile pickings.

In common with other asset classes, what has fuelled returns from property markets has been the same engine that has driven other assets, namely the secular decline in global interest rates. In property terms it manifested itself in the past five years or so in the form of yield compression.* With global interest rates turning and initial yields in most major markets dropping significantly in recent years, it is likely that most of the yield compression is behind us and rental growth will be the engine for returns from property investment. For the private investor markets that now display 'negative yield gap', where the cost of borrowing exceeds the initial retail yield, my advice is stay clear as institutional investors who don't or can't use leverage are better positioned to compete – unless of course you find a deal that has something very specific to attract you.

Hedge Funds and Managed Futures

The most important characteristic of hedge funds for the typical private investor, to my mind, is its lack of correlation with other asset classes. In general it tends to perform in a different fashion to the other classes, making it an excellent element as part of a wider portfolio. On their own they are either too expensive (fund of funds) or run the risk of losing everything, so use them sparingly. Expect predictable 4–6 per cent returns from fund of funds, but a charming stability! My best estimate is that they should form circa 12–15 per cent of your portfolio.

Private Equity and Commodities

For those who want to add some sparkle and some cocktail party conversation pieces to their portfolio, private equity investing and commodities might do the trick. Depend on them not to generate positive values for a number of years – that is their nature. Don't depend on them to deliver, but if they do, be ready to be sanctimonious and annoy all your friends with stories of your prowess. At most allocate about 5 per cent.

A portfolio with that type of make-up is far more likely to withstand a variety of investment environments and protect your wealth for the long run and into the next generation.

---

* Yield compression occurs when the yield on a property reduces as the capital value rises.

2.10. Asset Class Almanac 2007

If you use this as a basic portfolio, you can then start to 'tweek' the components depending on your objectives. Section 3.1 begins the discussion on how to set about this.

So what is different about this advice? Firstly it does not rest on one asset class and is more broadly diversified than is generally the case with a lot of pension funds for instance. Secondly, it includes a higher level of illiquid assets – property, private equity and so on than would be the case for non-private investors. Thirdly, it does recommend leverage and short selling as tools, either explicitly within your property portfolio or implicitly in hedge funds. Fourthly, it assumes that no one asset class has a fairer tailwind – there will be no free lunch from a secular downward trend in interest rates and consequently simply 'being in the market' won't be sufficient.

Investor's Almanac for the Coming Generation

The basic portfolio described above has provided remarkable stability to investors over a long period of time – the added diversity even saw it preserve wealth during the worst of the recent bear market. That sort of predictability is worthwhile. But be warned – even diversity of this kind cannot withstand seismic shifts in the underlying economy. Arguably one such shift is underway at present. In steps with little more visibility than the movement of tectonic plates, we are seeing the end of the disinflation begun by Reagan, Volcker, Thatcher and, more locally, Haughey and maintained by Clinton, Greenspan, Blair and, more locally, Ahern and McCreevy and the beginnings of a new era in which budget deficits, borrowing and rising interest rates will come to feature and the emerging Chinese economy will re-write global capital flows.

From an investor's perspective it is very helpful to understand where geo-politics might bring us in getting one's bearings in the market. Right now investors should pay particular attention to the role that government tends to play. Some commentators argue that the past two decades or so have been a 'bull market in markets' and that we are now entering a 'bull market in government'. The last time that the world saw a 'bull market in government' was in the 1960s and 1970s. This last phase of governmental growth came to an end, some argue, around the time Charles Haughey was on television telling us to tighten our belts, Margaret Thatcher was arguing there was no such thing as 'society' and Jimmy Carter appeared on US TV in a cardigan, telling Americans to save fuel by turning down the heat and putting on a jumper. The bull market in government had been inflationary in nature as, in particular, fiscal policy was loosened and governments borrowed to spend big. The problem was that it had driven the capital markets into a downward spiral ultimately resulting in 'stagflation', a problem that would create an equal and opposite reaction and effectively giving birth to the bull market in capital. In the US, the Fed chairman Paul Volcker put the American economy into recession as monetary policy was used to reign in excessive inflation. By the 1990s the profligacy had been reversed to the extent that conventional fiscal policy was to avoid deficits and indeed aim for surpluses. In addition, de-regulation became the *modus operandi* of many Western governments. As inflation was squeezed out of the system, monetary policy turned to supporting a generation-long secular reduction in interest rates – interestingly, towards levels of normality if one looks at interest rates over very long periods of time. The competitive urge underpinning the capital-friendly system itself unleashed a disinflationary process on the world economy and consequently asset prices rose dramatically.

At the start of this process, say in 1981, success in long-term investing meant having the foresight to see these trends and turning them into a real asset allocation plan. The assets that would benefit most would be financial assets (equities and bonds) as the key to their long-term valuation is interest rates. Equally countries with advanced market systems would outpace those where the 'cult of the equity' was less accommodating (so the US markets and its currency were healthy places to be).

Given that the situation for 2007 appears to be one where the disinflationary process is finishing and we are entering a modestly inflationary environment, in which it is quite possible that governments will once again play a bigger role at least for a period, it is rational to consider that the bases for a sensible asset allocation may have also changed.

It would be very foolish to extrapolate the lessons of the past directly but equally foolish to ignore this change. I would hazard the following as to what may be appropriate:

- Equities, though still important, will play a less significant role in this rising interest rate environment. In the immediate term, being relatively undervalued compared to other assets, equities should outperform. In the longer run there is likely to be much greater limits on the gains to be made.

2.10 Asset Class Almanac 2007

- Major indices may struggle to make significant gains, making index tracking a decidedly less rewarding activity and making active trading of equities much more valuable. That said, efficient developed markets may continue to provide a challenge for the active investor.
- Physical assets, whether property or commodities, will play a more significant role as a source of returns for investors. That's not to suggest that either will be a one-way bet as, in the short term, these markets too will fall foul of excess capital. Longer term investors will access the 'China/India' phenomenon from exposure to commodity markets.
- Leverage, though more useful in a low interest rate, low return environment, should be used more judiciously as credit default levels rise. With higher interest rates the level of leverage applied by investors needs to be more cautiously considered.

So what's wrong with this analysis? Probably one variable can re-write this – the extent of the emergence of China and India. An increase in their pace of growth (meaning the export of cheap labour) could ultimately lead to the export of more deflationary pressures than inflationary, which may serve to prolong the period in which inflationary pressures are offset. The Chinese currency in particular and the continuation of the mutual accommodation between the dollar and China will be the critical pressure valve that will determine how this plays out. Both countries have a mutual self interest in ensuring that there is no dramatic overnight devaluation of the dollar or mass exit from US securities. I would bet on this mutual, assured self interest (sometimes called the 'Bretton Woods II Agreement') that will ensure the process is a gradual one.

NOTES

1. 'Closing the Gap between Expected and Possible Returns', *AIMR Conference Proceedings: Integrating Hedge Funds into a Private Wealth Strategy* (Feb 2004), Vol. 2004, No. 1, CFA Institute, pp. 33–42.
2. 13 August 1979.
3. (1986), *De la Démocratie en Amérique* I (Bouquins), France: Robert Laffont, p. 171.
4. (1976), 'The Arbitrage Theory of Capital Asset Pricing', *Journal of Economic Theory*, Vol. 13, No. 3, pp. 341–360.
5. (2005), 'Perspectives on the Equity Risk Premium', *Bold Thinking on Investment Management*, CFA Institute, pp. 202–217.
6. (1999), *The Equity Risk Premium: The Long-Run Future of the Stock Market*, New York: John Wiley & Sons.
7. 'The Equity Premium', *Journal of Finance* (April 2002), Vol. 57, No. 2, pp. 637–659.
8. (2001), 'The Death of the Risk Premium: Consequences of the 1990s', *Journal of Portfolio Management* (Spring), Vol. 27, No. 3, pp. 61–74.
9. Ibid.
10. BNP Paribas 'The Inflationary Threat', May 2004.
11. Ibid.
12. Gregory Chun and James Shilling (1998) 'Real Estate Allocations and International Real Estate Markets', *Journal of Asian Real Estate Society*, Vol. 1, No. 1, pp 17–44.
13. Jones Lang La Salle (London), 'Rising Urban Stars – Uncovering Future Winners', May 2003, p. 3
14. 'Why Real Estate', *Journal of Portfolio Management*, Vol. 28, No. 1, pp. 20–32.
15. 'Real Estate – How much of their portfolio should European pensions funds allocate to real estate?' October 2005.
16. (2000), *Property Management*, Vol. 18, No. 1, pp 25–33.
17. Steven Rothwell (2006), 'Junk Bonds Rise in Europe', *Bloomberg News*, 3 November 2006 <http://www.iht.com/articles/2006/11/02/bloomberg/bxjunk.php>, accessed 11/11/2006.

Notes

18. Matthew Bishop (2004), 'The New Kings of Capitalism, a Survey of Private Equity', *Economist*, 27 November 2004.
19. Almeida Capital, *European Fundraising Review 2005*, <http://www.altassets.net/2006frreview.php>, accessed 4/11/2006.
20. 'Global Private Equity Report 2005', <http://www.pwcmoneytree.com/moneytree/index.jsp>, accessed 13/11/06, p. 12.
21. AltAssets (2004), 'US venture capital overhang reaches $68bn', <http://www.altassets.net/news/arc/2004/nz4583.php>, accessed 04/11/2006.
22. Lashinsky, Adam (2006), 'Private Equity's Barbarians are on Top – for Now', *Fortune,* 8 August 2006, <http://money.cnn.com/magazines/fortune/fortune_archive/2006/08/21/8383637/>, accessed 11/11/2006.
23. 'Fashions in Forecasting', *Fortune*, March 1949, pp. 88–91, 180–186.
24. Julie Rohrer (1986), 'The Red Hot World of Julian Robertson', *Institutional Investor*, May 1986, pp 86–92.
25. Kevin Muehring (1996), 'John Meriwether by the Numbers: Long-term capital management results moves fund into top ranks and founder's status has grown', *Institutional Investor*, Vol. 30, No. 11, pp. 37–46.
26. 'Barclay Group Estimate of Money under management by CTAs' <http://www.barclaygrp.com/>.
27. 'Who Should Buy Hedge Funds?' *ISMA Discussion Papers in Finance 2002–6*, ISMA Centre, University of Reading, 18 March 2002.
28. (2002), 'Hedge Fund Performance 1990–2000 – Do the money machines really add value?' *Alternative Investment Research Centre Working Paper Series No. 8*, Working Paper 1, 4 January 2002, Cass Business School, London.
29. (2004), 'Including Hedge Funds in Private Client Portfolios' *AIMR Conference Proceedings* (Feb 2004), Vol. 2004, No. 1, pp. 6–20.

PART II

PUTTING YOUR PLANS IN PLACE

CHAPTER 3

Asset Pools and Acronyms

3.1 Tax Treatments of Assets in Personal and Business Structures

As if getting to grips with each asset class wasn't confusing enough the next part of the wealth management process, principally tax, can get even more confusing. This is why thinking about your wealth in terms of 'pools of assets' is a useful way to simplify things.

An 'asset pool' is a pretty straightforward idea. It is simply a portion of your wealth that is dedicated to the achievement of a specific objective, and is generally taxed in a specific manner. By thinking about your investment strategies in this fashion, you can begin to break down the fog in your portfolio.

Asset pools come in all shapes and sizes, but I think that it is possible to generalise them into five areas:

1. Retirement Planning Pool

Your retirement planning pool will generally include the funds that will be used to generate an income in your retirement and will, usually, be invested in some form of tax-exempt pension fund, attracting tax relief. The objectives can be very easily quantified:

- What salary are you going to be looking to replace once you retire?
- How large a fund will you need to build to generate such an income?
- What risks are you prepared to take to make this a reality? (Alternatively put, what odds would you be prepared to gamble on not getting to your target income in retirement?)

If that sounds easy to calculate, you are mistaken. A lot of variables can put you a very long way off target. What if you retire early? What if stock markets take a tumble a couple of years before you retire (ask someone who wanted to retire in 2002 and was depending on the stock market)? What if your salary or employment status changes between now and retirement (it almost certainly will)? How fast will your current salary grow? How much inflation do you expect between now and retirement? What interest rate will apply when you retire (this could determine the amount of pension you can get from your accumulated fund)? In addition to that you have to consider the impact of your employment status. Some employments limit the pension you can fund for and, since the 2006 Finance Bill, the Government has put an overall limit on your pension fund size.

For many business owners, funding limits are a very important consideration and should be considered carefully. For example, in the case of occupational pension schemes, the typical pension fund is allowed to create an income in retirement worth two-thirds of the individual's final salary, where final salary is the average of the three highest consecutive salaries from the decade before retirement. In addition, provision can also be made for this income to continue to be paid to a surviving spouse on the death of the pensioner and all pensions in payment can be indexed in order to combat the impact of inflation. Obviously enough, the planning of your salary, your pension contributions and your final pension fund are inextricably linked.

Of course, the retirement assets pool is not constrained to pension funds – those simply happen to be the most tax-effective way to generate income in retirement. Once you reach retirement there may be other assets at your disposal which are more tax-efficient to use to generate an income (most DIRT-able deposits, gross-roll-up funds, net funds and CGT-able assets* can be first in line as a way of generating income as, for many retirees, the pension funds will attract marginal rate income tax).

As a general rule the sequencing of assets that should be used in retirement ahead of pension fund assets is as follows:

i. those assets that attract standard rate tax/DIRT but have no long-term potential to appreciate;
ii. assets where tax liability has been paid (e.g. net funds) but where there remains long-term potential for appreciation or where you might prefer to avoid selling in an unfavourable market;

---

* DIRT is Deposit Interest Retention Tax, currently 20/23% depending on the term of the deposit. Gross Roll-up is the tax applicable to funds and currently stands at 23%, comprised of standard rate tax +3%. CGT stands for Capital Gains Tax, currently 20%.

3.1 Tax Treatments of Assets

   iii. those assets that attract standard rate tax/DIRT but entail longer-term commitment if their potential is to be realised or if you prefer to avoid a forced sale in an unfavourable market;
   iv. those assets that are taxed under the gross roll-up regime;
   v. the ARF assets, as they will attract marginal rate tax and, after the Finance Act 2006, will be deemed to dispose of up to 3 per cent of their value every year.

2. Estate Planning Pool

For most people, the retirement planning tool is the most significant asset pool but increasingly it is far from the only one that is of importance in later life. In recent years, with the greater pace of wealth accumulation, the issue of estate planning has come increasingly to the fore. By separating those assets in your overall portfolio that you have earmarked either for your children or other family members, you can ensure that you are treating these in the most tax-efficient manner.

For example, a share portfolio of €200,000 that you might otherwise have sold off at retirement and used to generate income, might be better off left in mothballs in anticipation of capital appreciation over a longer period (say fifteen years). At that scale it might well suit as an inheritance for one of your children as it remains below their tax-free threshold for inheritance purposes.

3. Rainy-day Pool

I won't dwell on it. Most advisors suggest that it's useful to have between six and twelve months' income placed in cash or bonds where capital risk is modest and access can be immediate if so required.

4. Risk-taking Pool

Most business owners achieve their success from some element of personal risk-taking, whether they have felt the risk consciously or not. It tends to be one of the more common characteristics of successful business owners and it is one that they tend to take with them even after their business is sold and they are looking to enjoy the fruits of their labour.

This is why so many individuals get involved in funding start-ups and new business ventures or in investment adventures.

For some 'serial entrepreneurs' it's essential to the enjoyment of life to be involved in creating new value, whether that's through investment or new business ventures, and assets should be ear-marked for this activity.

5. Income Pool

No matter how successful you have been, if you have sold your business you will have to adjust to providing your income from your existing assets pool. This may sound like a simple matter but it's worth checking how much of your day-to-day expenses that were once caught up in the company and will now fall to your personal expenditure (take your car for example). What's more don't expect that, just because you're not working, your day-to-day expenditure will fall. When working, you probably spent most of your money on Saturday and Sunday (meals out, weekends away and so on). But when you are retired, every day in a sense is Saturday or Sunday.

The rationale for thinking in terms of assets pools is quite straightforward. It provides a convenient way to ring-fence each objective within your wider financial plans. In that way, what may be a short-term objective, such as meeting your income and expenses, can be balanced with some of the longer-term objectives such as a retirement or estate planning. The solutions that you deploy as a result may look very different also. You might not be prepared to face the risk that you won't be able to sell your business in five years and retire early to France, and as a consequence you may have to heavily fund for this objective in a relatively low-risk fashion. Conversely you may be happy that the investment strategy underpinning your retirement funds can be that bit riskier as if you don't believe that you'll need to access it for income for another fifteen years. Equally you may be happy to earmark high risk assets for your children's inheritance. The permutations are obviously endless, but the principles are pretty simple:

- set the objective you have in mind, in particular the time-frame;
- consider how much flexibility you are prepared to allow when it comes to meeting this objective;

- ring-fence the asset pool for that objective;
- ensure that the legal structure that you deploy is appropriate.

The resulting asset allocation decision that you apply to each asset pool should relate to your individual objective, with particular attention paid to the time frame. The overall resultant asset allocation that applies to all of your wealth is a by-product of these asset allocations.

3.2 Investment and Taxation for Business Owners

There are three perspectives that we must take in addressing how investing is taxed for the business owner:

Taxation of Investments in Personal Hands

Held in personal hands, an investment can be subject to capital gains tax, income tax, gross roll-up tax, net fund tax, PRSI or levies and eventually capital acquisitions tax. So the choice that you face at the outset, once an investment is to be made, can have a very substantial impact on the return you finally receive.

The principal areas to be aware of are:

Gross Roll-up Funds

The most common form of pooled investment funds these days are 'gross roll-up funds', so called as they allow both income and capital gains on a fund to be 'rolled-up', 'gross of tax'.

In effect what this means is that the fund pays neither income tax on income coming into the fund from securities it holds, nor capital gains on the appreciation in the price of those securities when they come to be sold. Instead these funds pay tax on exit, on the gain in the value of the fund at standard rate tax plus 3 per cent. Since 2006 these funds are subject to paying this tax every eight years on a 'deemed disposal' basis – meaning that the tax will come due whether you have encashed the funds or not (exactly 'how' this will work is still being considered).

Aside from this latter element, this system is relatively easy to administer and to understand from an investor's perspective and it makes it very transparent in terms of the final tax bill, not least because the financial institution has to take care of it on your behalf – if they are based in Ireland.* Non-Irish gross roll-up funds that can be invested in by Irish investors (such as funds in Luxembourg UCITS†) face the same taxation except that the obligation rests with the investor to inform the Revenue Commissioners that the investment has been made, when it is cashed in and to pay the tax liability.

One important element of gross roll-up funds that is important to bear in mind is the role that they can play in your estate planning. In the event of death, a gross roll-up fund may be transferred into an estate, and when the exit tax liability is met, the amount of tax paid can be offset against any inheritance tax liability.

These days most life assurance unit-linked funds, with profit bonds, unit trusts and investment companies are taxed in this fashion.

Net Funds

Net funds are the predecessors of the gross roll-up funds and a significant part of the assets managed by the fund industry continues to be invested in this fashion (although they attract a lot less new monies these days than their newer cousin).

In the hands of the investor, the tax liability is pretty simple – it isn't there any more. Instead the tax is paid by the fund on an ongoing basis. The rate of tax applied is the standard rate of tax, which applies to all gains and income on an ongoing basis. In practice the taxation of these funds is made slightly more complex by the fact that some years there are losses and some there are gains. This complexity is dealt with by spreading out the tax liability for any year over a number of years. All of the tax liability is handled within the fund by the manager so individual investors don't have anything left to do to take care of the tax bill.

---

* At time of writing the administration of eight years deemed disposal remains to be clarified.

† UCITS stands for Undertaking in Collective Investment in Transferable Securities.

3.2 Investment and Taxation for Business Owners

Taxation of Individual Shares/Bonds/Properties

Holding an individual share, bond or property can give rise to both a capital gains tax liability on any gain made due to price appreciation and an income tax liability at marginal rate on any income, whether that be dividends, rent or coupons generated by the investment.

Offshore Funds

Offshore funds created huge controversy in recent years and most investors are very wary of their use – and rightly so. Contrary to popular myth there is nothing illegal about investing in an offshore fund. What is illegal is using such funds to invest monies that have not paid appropriate taxes or failing to tell the Revenue that you hold the funds or that you have cashed them in. At this stage however, with the current Irish fund regime allowing gross roll-up of gains and income and applying just 23 per cent to profits, offshore funds have little appeal to most investors.

One rationale that I can see for investing in offshore funds is in the case of specialist investment strategies that may simply not be available within the Irish system or within a comparable EU gross roll-up regime (e.g. some specialist hedge funds are domiciled in the Caribbean, which would mean a marginal rate tax on an income or gains within such a fund for an Irish resident).

Taxation of Investment in Company Hands

Assets held in your company's ownership can create quite a different set of variables for you as an individual, particularly when it comes to taking the wealth out of the company structure and into your personal hands. In addition to the taxes that might apply above, you also have to consider the impacts of corporation tax, the close company surcharge and income tax on dividends, salary or bonuses.

A significant number of business owners make the mistake of retaining the bulk of their assets within corporate structures with the result that they can face unnecessary taxation before being able to access the fruits of their labours.

Tax-exempt Investing

The 'last great tax break' comes in the form of tax relief available on pension contributions, which in turn builds into tax-exempt pension funds. As a business owner or self-employed professional you are probably familiar with the annual paper bombardment from the financial services industry as the massed ranks of financial marketers vie for space in your pensions shopping cart. 'Top performers over ten years' compete with 'top performers over five years' who in turn go toe-to-toe with 'most consistent performer' and 'most awards won this year'. For those who are dismissive of competition in the sector, ask anyone who has worked in a pension fund manager whose performance came in at the bottom of the league table, especially if this continued for a prolonged period.

Despite the annual beauty pageant, the benefits of tax-exempt investing should be obvious to all. Tax relief at marginal rate for an individual, at corporate tax rates for companies and tax exemption from capital gains tax, corporation tax and income tax (it does not exempt schemes from other taxes such as VAT or Stamp Duty) all make a very compelling case for making maximum use of the pension system. Section 3.3 deals with some of this system's splendid acronyms, at least those that have more relevance to the business owner.

3.3 The Case for Personal Pensions, Executive Pensions, Company Pensions, AVCs, Annuities, ARFs, SSAPs and PRSAs

In anyone's book, except perhaps that of a fiscally challenged government, reducing a tax bill is a desirable outcome. Equally when one considers the extent to which our ageing population needs to be mindful of how it will look after its retirement, it is little wonder that the Government sees fit to provide generous tax relief and incentives for individuals to make provision for their later years.

If it were only simply understood and less riddled with clichéd complexity, I believe that the pension system would feature to an even greater extent in the country's daily discourse and more prominently in the political agenda. It should be – it is quite possibly – the single most important long-term issue facing Europe as a whole as we career into a demographic difficulty of a kind never seen before.

3.3 The Case for Personal Pensions

It is all the more important for business owners whose fate is quite literally completely in their own hands. By the time many of today's entrepreneurs do retire, the extent to which Europe will be weighed under by the pensions issue will be nothing short of breathtaking. Ireland has already taken far-sighted action in the form of the National Pensions Reserve Fund and is to be applauded for resisting the temptation to plunder this for shorter-term needs. This advance funding by the State is designed to partially support future Social Welfare pension payments and the future pension payments of civil servants (both of which currently operate on a pay-as-you-go basis).

Few issues affect business owners in the manner that pensions can. Firstly, pensions present a cost to your business and a legal duty of care that you have to your employees, most notably since the introduction of PRSAs.* Secondly, they are an area in which you are left essentially to fend for yourself. As the owner of your own company, whether self-employed or a proprietary director, you have to take care of providing for your own retirement. To help you make the most of this there is generous tax relief available both for you and your company. What's more, in many instances, the pension system will provide you with one of the most tax-effective ways of transferring your wealth out of your company and into your personal ownership. In short, business owners ignore the benefits of the pensions system at their peril and need to be aware of how to use the pension system to optimum effect.

So what is a Pension and how might it be of use in Financial Planning for a Business Owner?

In general a pension scheme is a contract, trust or fund established to create a value for a person on their retirement, which in turn is available to them in retirement to provide an income. It is a very wide field encompassing large occupational schemes, state schemes, executive schemes, small self-administered schemes, etc. For the purposes of this book, and indeed some brevity, I will confine myself to discussing those pensions of relevance to the business owner, in particular executive pensions, SSAPs, PRSAs, personal pensions, AVCs and finally ARFs and annuities (for explanations of these terms, see below).

---

* Personal Retirement Savings Accounts.

Personal Pensions

The simplest form of pension is the personal pension, governed by the Tax Consolidation Act 1997 and suited mainly to the self-employed and the professional. Issued by insurance companies (with a small number of exceptions where trust-based schemes have been established for certain professions), the personal pension is a savings plan that attracts tax relief at the individual's marginal rate of tax.

To be eligible for a personal pension you must have taxable earnings arising under Case 1 and 2 of Schedule D (i.e. self-employed income from a trade or profession) or alternatively have non-pensionable income under Schedule E. Personal pensions are specifically designed for individuals and cannot be effected by companies (although a company can make a contribution on behalf of an employee in some circumstances). Neither can personal pensions be established for a person who has only investment income (including rental income) or who is outside of the Irish tax jurisdiction.

Underlying the insurance contracts available to investors is an array of unit funds ranging from simple cash funds, through most of the major asset classes (equities, bonds and property) to with-profit funds and the popular managed funds. More recently, personal pensions have invested in unit funds that in turn have borrowed to purchase individual properties (subject to some restrictions).

Prior to April 1999, there was no absolute limit on the amount of tax relief that could be claimed in respect of contributions to a personal pension plan (other than mainly being limited to 15 per cent of net relevant earnings). However since April 1999, the tax relief varies according to age, as shown in Table 3.1.

In addition, a cap on the amount of net relevant earnings that can be included for the purpose of calculating contribution relief was introduced. This cap is currently €254,000.

Table 3.1: Eligible Earnings for Tax Relief

Age	% of Net Relevant Earnings
Under 30	15%
30–39	20%
40–49	25%
50 and over	30%

3.3 The Case for Personal Pensions

Interestingly however, personal pension plans do not come with a limit on the amount that can be contributed, only the amount that will attract tax relief, so significantly higher investments can be made.

Executive Pensions

Executive pensions by contrast are occupational pension schemes often established by an employer with a life assurance company to build retirement benefits for its proprietary directors or senior employees. As occupational schemes, both the individual and the company can make contributions to the scheme. In so doing the company can write off its contributions as an expense and the individual can get tax relief on any contributions they make in a personal capacity (subject to the same limits as outlined above for personal pensions).

For the business owner, executive pensions make for a particularly effective way to manage cash from your company balance sheet into your personal ownership. By getting your company to make contributions to an executive pension plan, your company gets to write off the expense plus the funds leave the company's ownership without any tax consequence. Once in the scheme they grow tax free until you retire, at which point you face a number of choices (see section below on Approved Retirement Funds). It represents a significantly more attractive approach in comparison to any other alternative such as paying cash as salary or in dividends.

The limit on contributions that can attract tax relief to an executive (occupational) scheme is the same as that which applies to personal pensions or PRSAs (15–30 per cent depending on age). The amount that can be contributed by the company is not limited in this fashion. What has been limited is the scale of the pension fund itself. In the Finance Act 2006, the scale of a pension fund has been restricted to €5m on retirement, indexed from this year. The indexation component is vital – assuming that earnings grow by 3 per cent over the next twenty years, this limits the fund to €9m on that person's retirement.

Additionally, the scheme itself is limited by not being allowed funds for an income on retirement of greater than 66 per cent of the employee's final earnings (with final earnings estimated as the average of the highest three consecutive years in the last ten years prior to retirement). 'Earnings' for this purpose include all elements of an employee's remuneration package

Table 3.2: Estimated Maximum Contribution Rates

Age at start	Retirement Age 60	Retirement Age 65
40	75% of earnings	51% of earnings
45	100% of earnings	65% of earnings
50	150% of earnings	88% of earnings
55	290% of earnings	132% of earnings

Note: These rates are purely indicative.

which are liable to tax under Schedule E (including benefit-in-kind). It should also be noted that in order to fund for the maximum pension of 66 per cent of final earnings, one must complete at least ten years service with the company by retirement age.

The total level of annual contribution capable of being invested can be very significant, depending on your age at the start and your proposed retirement age. In Table 3.2 I have set out some estimated contribution rates based on funding for revenue maximum benefits.

The revenue maximum benefits taken are a member's pension of two-thirds final earnings, a spouse's pension of 100 per cent of the member's pension payable on the member's death in retirement and indexation of pensions in payment at 3 per cent per annum.

Investing in Property through Personal and Executive Pensions
Both personal and executive pension funds can invest directly in property through unit funds, either with or without borrowing. As pooled investments this usually means that you won't have the flexibility to select your individual property within such a scheme but will be investing as part of a group of at least ten investors. Many life offices now provide investment for commercial and residential property schemes via such contracts (often referred to as geared pension property funds).

Small Self-Administered Pensions (SSAPs)

The Finance Act 2004 created a lot of talk about small self-administered pensions (SSAPs). SSAPs, as the name suggests, are small schemes that cater for less than twelve members. Sharing all the features of occupational schemes save their size, SSAPs are also subject to a series

3.3 The Case for Personal Pensions

of additional rules that limit their application somewhat. Principal amongst the limitations are:

- SSAP investments must be at arm's length to the beneficiary (so you can't buy your factory as an asset of your SSAP).
- The investments cannot be for personal use (so the holiday home is not allowed).
- You cannot invest in 'pride in possession' articles (so the yacht stays where it is).

Importantly since the Finance Act 2004, the SSAP is allowed to borrow as part of its investment strategy, making it a flexible vehicle in which to hold investment properties and through which to select the property you wish to purchase. Probably the most appropriate circumstances for such an arrangement are:

- where you are investing in commercial property, bought from and let to a third party;
- where the loan is completely self-financing (which may limit the amount of borrowing that can be available);
- where it is unlikely that you are going to draw an income immediately on retirement, in that you propose to transfer the property into your approved retirement fund.

Aside from these circumstances, in general, SSAPs may not be the most effective vehicle when compared to other pension arrangements. With the introduction of a cap on pension fund sizes in the Finance Act 2006, effectively this will limit the use of SSAPs to more modest individual properties – arguably to a point where the pension fund may not be sufficiently diversified.

Importantly any investor considering deploying gearing within a pension fund needs to appreciate the extent of the risk that this entails. The impact may be to magnify either gains or losses – the fact that one is deploying a bank's capital simply serves to ensure that there is a fixed amount that must be repaid.

When these changes came into effect in 2004 there was an expectation that SSAP's would become a hugely important part of the personal pensions industry. It was felt at the time that this would create an inflow of geared property transactions via such structures. However the effect of the limitation of €5m (indexed) introduced in 2006 was to constrain the types of property transaction very considerably.

Personal Retirement Savings Accounts (PRSAs)

Personal retirement savings accounts (PRSAs) were introduced into the pensions system after the passing of the Pensions (Amendment) Act 2002. They have much in common with personal pensions, not least of which being that they are set up under contract law, as opposed to the trusts that apply in much of the rest of the pension world. PRSAs are now available from all of the main financial institutions, as in contrast to personal pensions they can be issued by banks, building societies, investment businesses and stockbrokers.

Designed to ensure that the use of pensions increased significantly, PRSAs come in standard and non-standard versions and in an AVC (additional voluntary contribution) version. Standard PRSAs tend to have limited investment options and have capped charges, whereas non-standard PRSAs tend to have a wider range of investment options and have no cap on the level of charges.

PRSA contracts permit contributions to be made by individuals or indeed by their by employers. The legislation generally requires all employers to make PRSA facilities available to their employees (where no pension scheme is already up and running, or where access is limited or where there is a waiting period restricting access greater than six months).

The types of investment that can be undertaken by PRSAs are similar to that available through personal pensions. Each PRSA provider is required to provide a default investment strategy and investment is generally limited to pooled investments such as unit trusts, UCITS, insurance funds or investment companies where appropriate diversification of risk is achieved, sufficient liquidity is available, charges are identifiable and pricing is frequent and published. The legislation on standard PRSAs is quite specific about charges, placing a charging limit of 5 per cent on contributions and 1 per cent per annum on management fees. Arguably one of the advantages of PRSAs is this clarity in charging, as the legislation is quite specific about what has to be included in the charges and prohibits some of the more imaginative charging arrangements that apply if an investor suspends or changes their contributions. Nonetheless, the limits on standard PRSA charges are very similar to the level that applies to most personal pensions and executive pensions.

Approved Retirement Funds (ARFs)

The Finance Act 1999 introduced a new concept into financial planning in Ireland which is of immense importance to individual business owners: the Approved Retirement Fund. This presents new options as to how to use your pension fund when you retire in order to provide an income.

Before I continue, it's important to note that an Approved Retirement Fund is presently only available on retirement to:

- directors who own or control more than 5 per cent of the share capital of the company;
- personal pensions holders;
- individuals who have made AVC contributions either to an employer scheme or a separate AVC scheme;
- PRSA holders.

So it's not open to everyone, but it does have a potentially wide application in the future.

Prior to 1999, once you reached retirement age, you had but one decision to make when it came to your pension fund – from which life assurance company should you buy your annuity? An annuity is a financial contract under which you are paid a pre-determined income in retirement for as long as you live. With low interest rates, many people argued that annuities represented poor value for money and what's more you only stood to 'win' if you were one of the lucky ones who survived longer than average after retiring. A guaranteed income yes, but a game of chance between you and the insurance company nonetheless. If you passed away a few months after retirement, the life assurance company potentially pocketed your fund (unless you included provision for the pension to continue to a surviving spouse). On the other hand, if you survived forty years, it ended up costing the insurance company.

On retirement, you are entitled to 25 per cent of the value of the fund free of tax that has been built up in the personal pension, PRSA, executive pension or SSAP, free of tax. Advice with this aspect of pensions planning is simple – take the tax-free lump sum! That done, the choices are much greater as, instead of being forced to purchase an annuity, the retiree can now opt to retain ownership of their pension fund assets in an approved retirement fund. Such a fund can invest in a similar manner to that of a pension fund (although it cannot borrow directly).

The introduction of the Approved Retirement Fund, however, potentially provides a more attractive facility and greater flexibility as to how to use the remaining 75 per cent.

The amount that you can transfer is only restricted if your pension income in retirement does not exceed €12,700 per annum. As a retiring and successful business owner, one hopes that this restriction will not be applicable, but if it is the restriction is that you are obliged to place the first €63,500 into an approved minimum retirement fund, the capital of which cannot be accessed prior to age seventy-five.

At first glance, the Approved Retirement Fund is immensely attractive, in comparison to the apparently more restrictive annuity option. There are little restrictions on how your ARF may be invested and all the conventional choices remain open to you. However there is a significant distinction of which you should be aware before leaping into such an arrangement: there is no 'insurance' against you outliving your funds.

The one clear advantage that an annuity displays is the inbuilt insurance against longevity. In a paper published in November 2000 the Society of Actuaries in Ireland estimated that there is a 50–60 per cent chance that funds would be depleted by an individual taking a regular income before they died.[1] So for an individual who has the good fortune or good health to live into their nineties the odds of an ARF still generating income may not be as high as one might think at sixty or sixty-five. With an annuity, in contrast, you are guaranteed the agreed income for life – no matter how long you live.

And it is worth remembering that the average life expectancy for a male retiring at age sixty-five is now almost nineteen years (bringing you up to age eighty-four) and for a female the average life expectancy is circa twenty-two years, taking you to eighty-seven.

Prior to 2006, ARFs also provided the capability to transfer wealth inter-generationally in a quite tax-effective fashion. By leaving funds untouched in an ARF, the value grew free of tax and on death could be transferred to an estate and face conventional Capital Acquisitions Tax liabilities. This facility remains in place but has been constrained by the

3.3 The Case for Personal Pensions

Finance Act 2006, which introduced what is termed a 'deemed disposal'. With effect from 2006, an ARF is deemed to have disposed of a modest amount in income each year – starting with 1 per cent in 2006 and rising to 3 per cent from 2008 onwards. The effect of this is to reduce, although not remove, the tax attractiveness of ARFs for individuals who did not wish to use the vehicle immediately to generate income.

Assessing Income Needs
The extent of your income requirements in retirement is a critical consideration when looking to decide on an investment in approved retirement funds. If you have amassed a small fund and have significant income requirements, you may find you run a very big risk of depleting your assets very quickly. If you have other investments, particularly ones that are taxed at lower rates (such as gross roll-up funds or net funds) these should be used in advance of using ARFs as ARFs will attract marginal rate tax.

Future Asset Returns
While we've discussed this at length in the first section of the book, it's worth remembering that the prospects for double digit returns in the current environment – in the long run – are pretty poor. In such circumstances it might well be either brave or foolhardy to run a high level of income from an ARF without having alternative sources of income.

Are ARFs the Panacea?
There is no simple answer to the question of whether ARFs or annuities are 'better', particularly after the changes in the Finance Act 2006. It depends on each individual's circumstances and your advisor should guide you through this. As part of the decision making process, one needs to consider:

- What are your income requirements in retirement?
- Do you have other income? (e.g. rental income, dividends etc.)
- What dependents do you have?
- Will you need to draw on the ARF funds (aside from the obligatory amounts) or do you intend to leave this fund as an inheritance?
- What is your state of health (and that of your spouse)?
- What level of investment risk are you comfortable with?

Depending on your answers there are advantages and disadvantages to both ARFs and annuities.

Advantages of an annuity:

- A guaranteed income for life.
- Can be continued to a surviving spouse.
- Can be indexed to inflation.
- Provision can be made for an annuity to be paid for a minimum period of up to ten years irrespective of how long you live.

Disadvantages of an annuity:

- The capital must be ceded to the assurance company providing the annuity.
- In a low interest rate environment the annuity may appear to represent poor value.
- Income is fixed at a date of purchase and cannot be varied subsequently (other than if indexation is built into the annuity).
- Capital is lost on death (other than if provision is made for a spouse's pension or a pension guarantee is provided for).
- Cannot be left as an inheritance to children.

Advantages of an ARF:

- You retain control of the capital.
- You decide how much and when to draw income from the fund, allowing for a minimum of 3 per cent 'deemed disposal' following the Finance Act of 2006.
- Any capital remaining on your death goes to your next of kin. Initially your spouse (if surviving) can take over the ARF and, on their death, any residual can go to the children.

Disadvantages of the ARF:

- The ARF does not guarantee income in retirement.
- Depending on the investment return earned by the fund, the rate of income drawdown and how long you live, you could 'exhaust' the fund while you're still alive.

3.3 The Case for Personal Pensions

- Since the Finance Act 2006, it is assumed that you draw income from the ARF and this 'deemed disposal' creates a liability for Income Tax. The amount deemed to be disposed of is 1 per cent in 2006, 2 per cent in 2007 and 3 per cent in 2008 and thereafter.

In an interesting US analysis produced by Michael Lane in the *Journal of Retirement Planning*, the author offers a challenge to the conventional wisdom that buying an annuity is bad value for money based on these very reasons. He uses some of the concepts that we discussed in the first part of the book, including the outlook for the equity risk premium. His conclusion was that annuities have a role to play, as the risk is significantly greater of a fund investment depleting over time, and recommended that, in situations where an individual requires income in retirement, a fixed annuity should at least form part of the solution.[2]

I tend to agree with Lane's analysis if there is no other source of income in retirement. If other funds (e.g. net funds, gross-roll up funds or deposits) are available as the first source of assets to be depleted in the generation of income in retirement, then ARFs can indeed be the best route for transfer from the pension fund. However if the pension fund is the sole source of income and assuming that the low-return world we described in the first half of the book comes to pass, then it is likely that the pace of asset depletion may not always be adequate to maintain sufficient funds for those fortunate enough to live long into their ninth or tenth decade.

The Situation on Death

When you might die is the important part here. If it were to happen before your retire then, for a company director, a pension may pay out a lump sum of up to four times your final salary along with a dependent's annuity. If you make it beyond retirement, it all depends on how you invested the residual fund (after taking the tax-free lump sum). If your money is invested in an ARF then your spouse can take over the ARF on your death and when both of you have passed on, any capital remaining in the ARF goes to children, subject to tax at the standard rate. If, on the other hand, you invested some or all of the fund into an annuity, then it all depends on exactly what type of annuity you purchased, i.e. whether you bought an annuity with an attaching spouse's annuity and/or whether you built in a guarantee that the annuity would be paid for a minimum period (say five or ten years) irrespective of your survival.

Estate Planning

When it comes to planning your estate, ARFs have a clear advantage: the contributions will have been extracted from your company tax effectively; the funds built up in the pension fund will have grown tax-free; you will have had the opportunity to access one quarter of the total fund tax-free on retirement and then the full value remaining can pass through to your spouse and then your estate on your death – an attractive round trip from a tax perspective alone. The Finance Act 2006 has gone some way to reducing the attractiveness as you will have to take up to 3 per cent per annum in income every year from the ARF.

Take-Away Advice

The pension system that has developed in Ireland in recent years provides immense flexibility and highly attractive tax incentives. As a business owner, if you haven't yet used pension planning to your advantage, make sure to; it is one of the few 'no-brainers' in financial planning.

Make sure however that you are getting the right structure for your needs – in particular if you are using pensions in any way to purchase properties – as there are pitfalls, lots of them, and there are few other areas where specialist expertise is as valuable.

If you are nearing retirement make sure to start thinking about your ARF plans. In general ARFs are a valuable and very flexible approach to securing your income in retirement as well as providing an excellent method of retaining ownership in your personal hands. The downside to this can be controlled by keeping your income expectations in check. In addition, while many advisors would argue against it, I believe that annuities can continue to provide a bedrock part of your income in retirement, alongside ARFs.

NOTES

1. (2002), 'Retirement Options and Approved Retirement Funds', 26 November 2002, <http://www.actuaries.ie/Press%20Office/Briefing%20Statements/001126-BS_Retirement%20OptionsARFs.pdf>, accessed 14/10/2006.
2. (2001), 'Annuitization: An Eye-Opening Analysis', *The Journal of Retirement Planning*, May/June 2001.

CHAPTER 4

Personal Wealth Protection for Business Owners

4.1 A Reminder to put the CAT out

Capital Acquisition Tax (CAT) is payable where the value of any gift or inheritance exceeds certain values. The values, known as the tax-free threshold, depend on the relationship between the person making the gift/inheritance and the recipient. There is no CAT payable on gifts or inheritances between spouses. The CAT rate is currently 20 per cent payable by the recipient.

Tax-Free Thresholds

The tax-free thresholds in Table 4.1 apply in respect of gifts or inheritances taken on or after 5 December 1991.

This threshold between your child and yourself is a lifetime threshold and all gifts or inheritances from both parents since 5 December 1991 will be taken into account in determining the amount that they can receive before a tax liability is created.

Table 4.1: Tax-Free Thresholds 2007

Relationship of Beneficiary to Person Making Gift/Inheritance	Exempt Amount 2007
Child, minor child of a deceased child, parent taking inheritance.	€496,824
Grandparent, grandchild, brother, sister, niece, nephew, parent taking a gift.	€49,682
All others (includes non-marital partners, friends, in-laws).	€24,841

Disposal of Family Home

It's not always thought about but it's certainly worth noting that the gain on the disposal of your 'principal private residence' is potentially liable to capital gains tax (CGT). However, there is an exemption from CGT in relation to this disposal if the property has been occupied as your sole or main residence while you owned it and the land that goes with the house isn't greater than one acre.

If you haven't lived in the property while you owned it, then any gain will be apportioned. The element of the gain relating to the period of absence will be subject to CGT unless it falls within one of the following:

- periods of absence deemed to be periods of occupation;
- periods of absence throughout which you worked in an employment requiring you to work overseas;
- any period not exceeding four years throughout which you were prevented from residing in the dwelling house as a result of a condition imposed by your employer requiring you to reside elsewhere.

These periods will qualify only if you lived in the property as your sole or main residence before and after the period of absence.

The relief is also available to you on a gain arising to you on the disposal of a house which was used by a dependent relative as the relative's main residence. In allowing this, it is dependent on the relative living free of rent.

The exemption is not applicable where property has been purchased wholly or mainly for the purpose of making a gain on its disposal or to any part of the chargeable gain which reflects any 'development land value'.

Passing on a Family Business

As a business owner, chances are that some or all of your family are working in your business. Some may be directors and the very future viability of your business may rest with them once you have retired. Indeed the livelihoods of many of your employees may rest with the smooth management of the transfer of ownership of your business. Bad planning in the normal running of your business may damage it in the short term, but bad management of the ownership of your business can be fatal.

4.1 A Reminder to put the CAT out

Even aside from the good governance associated with planning your exit from the business it can also ensure what is many business owners' dream: to see their business continue to flourish in their family's hands into the next generation.

The safe transfer of your business to your children will have tax implications, of that there is no denying. However, there is specific relief available to deal with such transfers that can mitigate or indeed eliminate tax liabilities.

CAT, Business Property and Agricultural Relief

As a business owner, 'business property relief' can be a very significant part of your estate planning.

Business property relief reduces the value of a qualifying business property by up to 90 per cent (i.e. to 10 per cent) for CAT purposes (it's lower for inheritances made earlier than January 1997). Equally, agricultural relief reduces the value of agricultural property by 90 per cent before CAT is applied. Certain conditions must be met in both cases for this relief to apply.

For example, let's assume you have a business property worth €1m. Assuming that this meets the criteria for eligibility, the notional value can be reduced to €100,000 for purposes of assessing the CAT on a gift/inheritance. This in effect means that a CAT bill that might otherwise have been 20 per cent is reduced to just 2 per cent. That's a neat bit of tax mitigation!

Business property qualifying for this relief includes:

- property consisting of an unincorporated (e.g. sole trader) business or interest in a business;
- unquoted shares in a trading company or securities of a company provided that after the gift/inheritance the new owner controls more than 25 per cent of the voting rights **or**
- the company is under the control of the beneficiary and his relatives **or**
- you controlled over 10 per cent of the company's share capital and were either a full-time working director or employee of the company throughout the period of five years prior to the gift or inheritance;

- land, buildings, plant and machinery owned by you and used in company's business or controlled by you or by a partnership in which you are a partner;
- quoted shares or company securities owned by you prior to their being quoted.

To qualify for relief such assets must be simultaneously transferred with the shares in the company or interest in the partnership. The shares in the company and the interest in the partnership must also qualify as relevant business property.

In addition you or your spouse must own the asset for at least five years immediately prior to the date of the gift or two years in the case of an inheritance that is taken on your death.

This is a tricky area in that many slight variations can occur, particularly as certain business assets may not have been held for the requisite period for good reason. Your accountant or tax advisor will be best positioned to advise you on exactly what will and won't be eligible.

Here are some examples:

Replacement Property held for less than Required Period
Relief is available in certain circumstances where the relevant business property was held for less than the required period but it replaced other relevant business property.

Transfer of Inherited Business prior to Required Period
Relief is also available when the period of ownership is not met if you, having received a gift or inheritance qualifying for business property relief, died before the ownership period is completed.

'Clawback' on Sale or Compulsory Purchase
If property, which has qualified for business relief, is sold or compulsorily acquired within six years of the date of the gift or inheritance, the business relief is withdrawn. This 'clawback' does not arise if the property disposed of is replaced by another business property within one year.

Shares in the following typically do not qualify for business property relief:

- shares in non-resident companies;
- investment companies, unquoted shares;

4.1 A Reminder to put the CAT out

- quoted shares in most resident and non-resident companies;
- investment properties.

Other exclusions include:

- relief on that portion of the value of the shares in a company that derives from a subsidiary company that would not itself qualify for relief (e.g. a company that engages in land or share dealing);
- relief on the portion of the value of shares in a company or on an interest in a business that derives from an asset that was not in use for the purposes of the business for two years prior to gift or inheritance.

CGT Retirement Relief

If you plan to transfer ownership of the business when you retire then for your part you need to consider the capital gains tax (CGT) implications of so doing.

Whether or not your children purchase the business from you this will be seen as a sale that will be subject to CGT. However, generally speaking, where an individual of fifty-five years or older has owned and operated the business on a full-time basis for a period of ten years up until the date of the transfer then no CGT should apply to this disposal.

Capital gains tax retirement relief applies to an individual sole trader (which includes farmers), an individual partner in a partnership or an individual whose business interests are held in a company.

'Qualifying assets' that will be eligible for the relief include:

- business assets which have been used for the purposes of a trade, profession or employment **or**
- in the case of business interests held in a company, shares of a 'family company' that is a trading company **or**
- land used for the purposes of farming carried on by the individual or land, plant or machinery owned by an individual and used in a trade carried on by his family company, and transferred at the same time and to the same person as the shares in that company.

A 'family company' is defined within the following limitations:

- Not less than 25 per cent of the voting rights are controlled by the individual or not less than 10 per cent of the voting rights are controlled by the individual and more than 75 per cent (including the 10 per cent) are controlled by the individual's family.
- The individual has been a working director for at least a ten year period and a full-time working director for at least five of those years.
- If the assets are shares in a family company and the transfer of the assets to that company was the subject of incorporation relief from CGT, the period of direct ownership of the assets will be aggregated with the period of ownership of the shares, or the period during which the individual was a full-time working director, as may be appropriate.
- The individual must own the qualifying assets (apart from tangible movable property) for at least ten years prior to the date of the disposal. These must be his chargeable business assets throughout the ten year period ending with the disposal. The period of ownership of the taxpayer's spouse is taken into account as if it were a period of ownership of the taxpayer. Where assets were sold and the proceeds were reinvested in further qualifying assets, the period of ownership of the assets which were sold is taken into account as if it were a period of ownership of the replacement assets (provided that the conditions for 'rollover relief' were satisfied). If the qualifying assets are shares in a family company or land, plant or machinery used by a family company, then the individual must have been a working director of that company for ten years and full-time working director for five years.

Where the disposal is to a child of the individual there is no limit on the proceeds, or gain, which qualifies for the relief so all such disposals are free of CGT. The relief is clawed back if the child disposes of the qualifying assets within six years.

Where the disposal is to someone other than a child of the individual, relief will be given for the full amount of CGT where the proceeds are below €750,000 (increased from €500,000 in Budget 2007). Transfers of qualifying assets to a spouse, although not subject to CGT, will be included at market value when calculating the amount of proceeds received. If the qualifying asset is shares in a family company, the proceeds to be taken into account shall only be the portion that relates to the chargeable business assets of the company. For proceeds that exceed €750,000 marginal relief may apply whereby the maximum CGT payable isn't greater than half of the excess of the proceeds over this amount. It is important to note that the individual need not actually retire or dispose of all the relevant assets in order to qualify for the relief.

CAT Dwelling House Exemption

Another possibly useful way to mitigate CAT bills as a part of your estate planning is to make use of the dwelling house exemption. This enables you as a parent to set up each of your children with a home of their own, the value of which can fall outside of the CAT threshold.

This exemption is limited to gifts or inheritances of the family home (or other dwelling houses) where the following conditions are satisfied:

- The child has lived in the house as his only and main residence for three years immediately before the gift/inheritance was made.
- The child has no interest in any other dwelling house at the date of the gift/inheritance.
- Where the child is under fifty-five years of age, he must continue to live in that dwelling house for six years after the gift or inheritance.

Transfer of Site as a Gift

The transfer of a site by parent to child usually results in a potential capital gains tax liability. However, there is an exemption from CGT in certain situations.

Provided the market value of the site is below the tax-free threshold for a child and the child has not used the threshold amount previously, no CAT would be payable.

There is an exemption from CGT as well as from stamp duty where a parent transfers a site to a child to enable the child to build their own home. (This applies to disposals on or after 6 December 2000.)

The exemption applies to the transfer provided certain conditions are met:

- The market value of the site does not exceed €254,000.
- The transfer is for the purpose of enabling the child to construct his principal private residence.
- Once built the child must live in the house as his only or main residence for a period of three years.

A 'clawback' of the exemption will arise if the child disposes of the site without having built and lived in their home for at least three years.

In summary there is a lot that can be done to plan the transfer of your family and business wealth in a fashion that mitigates the CAT bill that your beneficiaries will face. However, in the Ireland of today, even meticulous planning will probably not be sufficient to eliminate the tax liability completely.

Section 73 Life Assurance Policy

Despite every relief provided, once you transfer across your wealth to your children, they may end up facing an unwanted bill that may result in the sale of assets that would not otherwise occur. Having exhausted all other avenues, examples of which are described in the preceding sections, there remains one alternative: the Section 73* (formerly Section 60) life assurance policy. This form of life assurance should be the very last method used to mitigate the liability and not, as some people mistakenly assume, the first.

A Section 73 policy provides life cover in the event of the death of the second of the lives assured to die. This means it pays out once the inheritance becomes an issue, i.e. when both father and mother have died. It provides a non-taxable lump sum that your children can use to clear or reduce any CAT liability arising on your estate.

What makes the Section 73 policy attractive is its tax efficiency as the sum payable on your death is exempt from inheritance tax in so far as it is used to pay a CAT liability (your other life assurance payments will be counted as part of your estate to calculate the tax due). Section 73 is also particularly useful where there are illiquid assets such as property or private equity shares, which your children might otherwise be forced to sell, irrespective of market conditions, to meet their tax liability.

---
* Section 73 CAT Act

The main catch is that the proceeds of the policy must be used within one year of death to meet a CAT liability in order to be non-taxable.

4.2 Preparing Personal and Corporate Wills

'Will now and Will often'

Okay, none of us want to write one. It's almost an admission of mortality and indeed of reaching 'a certain age'. However it is an essential part of every business owner's broader financial planning. Without one in place much of the estate planning that may help pass assets relatively intact from one generation to another may well prove useless.

Once you have a will completed, you should update it on a regular basis to allow for changing legislation and family circumstances. A new addition to your family, new arrangements with your business partners, even a new grandchild may all be appropriate 'triggers' to pay a visit to your solicitor. By maintaining an up-to-date will you can ensure that your estate will be wound up in accordance with your intentions with minimum delay and cost, avoiding confusion and dispute between family members. Just as importantly, your will affords you the opportunity to plan the tax efficient transfer of your assets on death.

If you have a Young Family

Most particularly if you have a young family, your wills should allow for the unlikely eventuality of you both dying before your children are old enough to inherit or indeed mature enough to manage their affairs prudently. To cater for such an eventuality, you can elect to include a 'discretionary trust' in your will that can stipulate how and indeed by whom your children are financially cared for until they reach an age specified by you when their inheritance can be distributed to them in its entirety. Once all the assets held in trust are paid out to your children before your youngest child reaches age twenty-one, there are no additional tax costs associated with a discretionary trust. A discretionary trust can be a useful way for you to ensure that your children's best interests are catered for. Of course they may not thank you until they are old enough to appreciate the thought! Your solicitor can also advise you on this area.

Gift now and Gift often

Gifting assets to your children is also a useful method of gradually transferring your wealth across to the next generation and mitigating the total tax bill that may ultimately arise. It can be especially appropriate when children grow older and more capable of responsibly handling assets.

There are three principal advantages to gifting to your children (or perhaps other younger relatives) during your lifetime:

- Your children have their tax-free threshold amount to utilise.
- Once gifted, the asset appreciates in the child's name directly.
- As the CAT Aggregation date of 5 December 1991 may be brought forward in future there's always the possibility that prior gifts may fall out of the CAT net altogether – though that's only idle speculation.

Of course no tax planning is ever that black and white. There can also be other tax implications to consider depending on the type of asset being transferred. For example, the gifting of property is regarded as a 'deemed disposal' for CGT purposes and therefore a CGT liability may arise. Stamp duty implications could and probably will also need to be considered.

It goes without saying that any transfer of assets to a child should be done in full knowledge that the asset has essentially 'flown the nest'. There is little valour in minimising a child's CAT liability and your lifestyle at the same time!

Personal and Corporate Wills

For most people in salaried positions, estate planning only begins to be an issue that features in their financial planning when they first begin to think of retirement. For the business owner it should feature much, much earlier. The reason being that your being knocked over by a LUAS in the morning means your family income and the livelihood of your employee could be jeopardised.

The personal side to your will is a very private matter that should spell out your wishes for the disposal of your estate. Your solicitor should advise you on framing it in a prudent fashion. However, when it comes to those assets that are business related, the matter is more complex and, particularly with larger businesses, the involvement of your solicitor, company accountant and other financial advisors are generally recommended. Making sure that the personal side of your will interacts in a complementary fashion with the business side is more complex than you might first think.

Assuming that your company can go on without you there are some simple things you need to decide.

Succession Planning

Your succession planning within the company is the first part of your plan that you need to address and is usually amongst the trickiest. Little Johnny, whose budding rugby career might be a source of great pride, may provide no guarantee that he's the right person to step into your shoes. Many business owners naturally look to their immediate heirs to run their business in the event of their death or retirement, but not many think about whether the heir is the best choice.

In planning your succession you need to be brutally honest about whom amongst your family or other beneficiaries is the best equipped to carry on your business in the best interest of all its stakeholders, i.e. the long-term well-being of your family and other shareholders, your staff, your clients and suppliers. Having determined who is most appropriate, you'll then face the issue that not all will be happy with the decision, which is where there is a need for both your personal will and corporate will to interact in the interests of fairness. Whatever works best in your situation, you should lay out your succession plan in a detailed document that accompanies your personal will, which should seek to explain proposed changes in management and/or ownership as well as any financing strategies that you may deploy.

Almost inevitably, solving this conundrum should involve some form of business life assurance.

If your business cannot go on without you, then your planning at this stage needs to be quite different. A document should accompany your will providing your beneficiaries with a road-map about the value of the business and – importantly – outlining potential buyers.

4.3 Protecting Your Family and Your Business

Depending on the nature of your business and the manner in which your succession planning is configured, any one of the major types of business protection assurance may be useful.

Partnership Assurance

In a partnership arrangement, each partner owns a share of the capital and goodwill of the partnership and takes a corresponding share in the profits. The sudden death of a partner can cause financial problems for the surviving partner(s):

- The partnership may be dissolved, unless there is a prior agreement to the contrary.
- The next-of-kin of the deceased partner may want to come into the business but the surviving partner(s) may not want this.
- Even if the next-of-kin are willing to sell their share of the business to the surviving partner(s), the surviving partner(s) may not have the cash readily available or the capacity to borrow at that time.

Partnership insurance can solve the above problem. The two key components of putting partnership insurance in place are:

- The partners enter into a legal agreement, a buy/sell agreement, under which they agree that on the death of a partner, the deceased partner's next-of-kin must sell the shares and the surviving partner(s) must buy the shares of the deceased partner.
- In order to ensure that the surviving partner(s) are in a financial position to buy the shares, each partner effects life assurance for a sum equal to the estimated value of their shareholding. This capital is then available to the surviving partner(s) to buy the shares of the deceased.

The life assurance cover can be arranged in one of two ways:

Life of Another

Under this structure each partner insures each of his fellow partner's lives for a value equal to the amount needed by that partner to buy out a deceased partner's share.

The advantages of this method are:

- There is a fair distribution of cost, in that the younger partners pay the higher premiums (by insuring the older lives) and the older partners pay the lower premiums (by insuring the younger lives).

4.3 Protecting Your Family and Your Business

This is equitable in that, from a mortality perspective, it is the younger partners who are more likely to benefit (the older partners being statistically more likely to die).
- The capital ends up in the correct hands on death i.e. the surviving partner(s).
- The sum assured is not taxable in the hands of the surviving partner(s).

However this approach also has some disadvantages, such as:

- If there are a number of partners, then a large number of policies are required, since each partner insures each of the other partners. This can be cumbersome.
- This structure lacks flexibility, particularly when a new partner comes on board. In such a circumstance all the policies have to be re-jigged.

Own Life in Trust

Under this approach each partner effects a policy on his own life for an amount equal to the estimated value of their shares. Each policy is arranged under trust for the benefit of the other partner(s). In this way, on the death of a partner, the sum assured is paid to the nominated trustees, who then pay the amount over to the surviving partners, who then use this to buy back the shares of the deceased partner.

The advantages of this approach are:

- The structure is simple. Each partner insures his own life.
- The structure is flexible in that it easily accommodates new partners.
- It provides funds in the right hands at the right time, i.e. the surviving partners get cash so that they can buy the deceased's shares.

The disadvantage of this approach is that there is not an equitable distribution of cost, in that the older partners pay a higher premium and the younger partners pay a lower premium. Older partners may have difficulties with this.

An alternative strategy, adopted increasingly by professional partnerships, is to write goodwill out of the practice. On the death of a partner, no payment is made to the estate of the deceased partner. Instead, the goodwill is said to accrue from one generation of partners to the next. This is known as 'automatic accrual of goodwill'. To compensate for this, the partners will agree to effect a 'Section 785' life assurance policy on their own life for an agreed level of cover. Section 785 premiums are tax deductible within the overall personal pension tax relief limits.

Retirement of a Partner

The same issue arises when dealing with the retirement of a partner. In professional partnerships where goodwill may accrue from one generation to the next, there will generally be a requirement on partners to contribute to a personal pension plan. This will be in lieu of receiving any benefit from the partnership on retiring.

Co-director's Assurance

The sudden death of a shareholder in a company can have a major impact, not just on the family of the deceased but also on the surviving shareholders.

- What will happen to the shareholding?
- Will one of the deceased's family seek to join the business?
- Can the family of the deceased turn the shareholding into cash?
- Will the surviving shareholders be in a position to buy back the shares or is there a risk that the shares could be sold externally?
- Have the shareholders an agreement in place as to what will happen to the shares when a shareholder dies?

Such uncertainty may not be in the interest of the company, the surviving shareholders or the family of the deceased. Without an agreement, the surviving shareholders could find that the family of the deceased want to take a seat on the board or perhaps worse, they intend to sell the shareholding to an external buyer. Alternatively the family of the deceased may find that they cannot easily turn the shareholding into cash (e.g. in a minority shareholding situation), or they may have to wait some time for the surviving shareholders to come up with the cash to buy the shares.

As a result, there is uncertainty on both sides. Ideally both sides would probably prefer some certainty as to what would happen in the event of the death of a shareholder.

There are essentially two ways that a shareholder protection arrangement can be structured:

Corporate Shareholder Protection

Under the corporate shareholder protection route it is the company who enters into an agreement with each shareholder to buy back the shares from the deceased shareholder (through their personal representative) on death. Equally it is the company that then effects the insurance cover and pays the premium. This arrangement is complex and is dependant on the company having the power to buy back its own shares (see articles of association). In addition the taxation implications of the buy-back will also need to be considered. It is beyond the scope of this book to deal with all the permutations, suffice to say that those concerned should seek professional advice.

Personal Shareholder Protection

The personal shareholder protection route is similar to that outlined above for partnership insurance. The shareholders can enter into a buy/sell agreement and they can arrange the life cover on a 'life of another' basis or an 'own life in trust' basis.

It is important to remember that for any form of shareholder protection insurance, the individual will have to submit to some form of underwriting (e.g. medical examination). If any of the shareholders are in poor health, then the cost of the life cover may be increased to reflect the extra risk or indeed cover may not be obtainable at all in some cases.

Keyman Assurance

In addition to partners and directors, most businesses have significant assets that walk out the door each evening. Strange how a company will insure the managing director's car and desk, but not the managing director! Keyman insurance is the form of life assurance used to cover this risk. A relatively common practice amongst US firms (one estimate stands at 25 per cent of firms in the US), it remains relatively uncommon in Ireland and the UK.

Of course 'valuing' the impact on profitability of the loss of a key member of staff is an impossible calculation. One industry rule of thumb that is used is to take the individual's salary and multiply it by ten, providing the person is not nearing retirement in which case it can be significantly less.

Should you add in Permanent Health Insurance and Serious Illness Cover?

Permanent Health Insurance

Permanent health insurance (PHI) is a form of life assurance that pays out, not on death, but when a person can no longer work due to an illness or an accident. Many corporate pension schemes provide this benefit to employees so, for most people, it is something that is usually confined to the report from the trustees every year or so. For the business owner, it makes a slightly more compelling case given the risk that they face. In the event of incapacity or ill health, a business owner's financial future may be far less well catered for, hence why many opt to take out individual PHI. At present two of the Irish life assurance companies offer such cover (although they differ in cost and the type of premiums payable).

However permanent health insurance is a relatively complex form of insurance and there are a number of areas to watch out for:

The 'Deferred Period'
Typically the contracts offer deferred periods of thirteen, twenty-six or fifty-two weeks, which means they don't begin to pay out replacement income until the deferred period of thirteen, twenty-six or fifty-two weeks is up. Obviously, the longer the deferred period, the cheaper the premium.

The 'Own'/'Any' Occupation
Certain occupations are restricted when it comes to PHI and the insurance only pays out in the event that you cannot do your own or any occupation

4.3 Protecting Your Family and Your Business

for which you are reasonably suited – a much more restrictive condition than simply not being able to do your own job.

'Proportionate Benefits'

All PHI contracts will seek to ensure that the beneficiary is not discouraged from seeking to do any work. This provides typically that if, having been disabled from their own occupation, a claimant takes up another lesser-paid occupation, then benefit can continue in proportion to the reduced earnings.

This is a worthwhile insurance for business owners to consider but beware of the small print.

Serious Illness Cover

Serious illness cover became a very popular form of insurance against 'dread diseases' such as cancer, heart disease, kidney failure, stroke and many others during the 1990s. This cover provides a payment of a capital sum on a person being diagnosed as suffering from or contracting any of the specified illnesses listed in the policy. It remains a useful insurance but has become increasingly expensive in recent years and the claims experience of most reinsurance companies has worsened. We might be surviving more of these illnesses than was originally thought possible!

Amongst the many wonderfully morbid phrases that the life assurance industry has given to the English language is 'accelerated death benefit', which is a variation of serious illness cover. This is a form of serious illness cover under which you effect both a life assurance and serious illness cover benefit at the same time but it pays out only once, either on death or in the event of being diagnosed with a specified illness. Arguably it makes for a cheaper form of insurance probably as, if you are going to die, it's quite likely to have been from something 'on the list'. It is important to stress that with serious illness cover there are many more restrictions and exclusions than with life assurance. In the case of life assurance you are either dead or alive (there is little room for doubt). With serious illness however, it depends on whether you satisfy the precise definitions of illness as written in the policy.

Despite the somewhat absurd description of this type of insurance, taken from the perspective of the business owner facing a serious personal illness, such a circumstance, particularly when it involves debts, can be a serious financial challenge. The merits of this insurance now hinge on whether it continues to offer value for money, but the 'accelerated' version is considerably more affordable.

4.4 Using Debt as a Tool in your Financial Planning

Debt/credit/lending/borrowing/gearing, call it what you will, it is always with us.

Amongst the most powerful of ingredients in any business owner's financial toolkit is the ability to borrow. Using someone else's capital, particularly at the low cost that it has been available in recent years, makes eminent sense and cannot be ignored when it comes to putting together your plans.

Equally, an imprudent, even gluttonous approach to borrowing can have savage consequences for an individual's personal wealth.

That much is obvious. What's more revealing is the answer to the question 'How much borrowing is a good thing?'

How Much Borrowing?

Economists argue that each individual household has a level of 'human capital' – human capital being a claim on a future income stream. Those who have invested in their education or who have built businesses tend to have the highest level of human capital. The income that they ultimately receive is a dividend of sorts.

It's an interesting concept insofar as it applies both to a person's asset allocation decisions and how much they borrow.

Obviously enough, the higher the human capital, the greater the income stream likely to accrue and the greater the risks an individual can sustain. This is simple enough, except when you consider that both the income stream and risky assets tend to be related in some fashion. This is the case particularly if the risky asset (equities) is also the source for a lot of the income stream. Hence why some argue that holding a large equity portfolio when one is in receipt only of a risky income stream is doubling the risks and one should diversify away from risky assets in such circumstances. This is compounded by the fact that risky asset returns are also positively correlated to risky income sources.

4.4 Using Debt as a Tool in your Financial Planning

In short, if you work for a quoted company and your income comes from this company it may make a lot of sense to diversify your wealth away from the fortunes of the company.

From the perspective of borrowing, this concept is also useful. It suggests that a young adult who has built their 'human capital' to its maximum should be leveraging off this capital to the maximum extent possible, whereas individuals who are more advanced in years should be considering consuming their wealth and hence should be reducing their levels of leverage. So a young, recently qualified consultant, who may not have reached their full earning capacity yet, but who in all probability will, should have a significant human capital to draw upon and should leverage accordingly. Conversely a successful business owner, who is looking to sell their business may be better starting to reduce their borrowing burden and, if appropriate to them, begin to consume their wealth.

Academic work in this area makes estimates, under certain constraining circumstances, of how much one should allocate to risky assets – equities – and how much financial wealth one should hold relative to one's income.

In their book *Strategic Asset Allocation*, John Y. Campbell and Luis M. Viceira suggest that:

- a person with thirty years to retirement with a modest risk aversion should allocate 35–59 per cent of their wealth to the equity market;
- a person with fifteen years to retirement with a similar risk aversion should allocate 28–47 per cent to the equity market;
- a person with five years to go should allocate 23–37 per cent of their wealth to the equity market;
- a person in retirement of similar disposition should allocate 20–32 per cent.

Their work is not nearly so prescriptive as I paint it here – my apologies to the authors – but the point is worth labouring. As one nears retirement it is useful to reduce the risk of a portfolio.

Translating this into how much one should borrow, suggests that young, educated would-be millionaires are the people who should be borrowing the most! However, while that may sit well with the labour economics theoretician, it is unlikely to curry much favour with the local lending institution whose principal concerns will be the extent of recourse to the borrower, the quality of the borrowing covenant and the means by which repayment is to be financed.

These are competing imperatives – hence the reason why, just as you probably need to borrow less, you'll find lenders willing to lend you more!

Some Rules of Thumb

I recall an accounting lecturer once claiming that 'current ratio' of assets to debt for a company would be optimised somewhere around 2:1. So if your total investable assets come to €2m, you should probably limit your debt at about €1m. That's providing you have income to also support that level of debt. I also encountered a banking rule of thumb that a debt repayment in excess of about 40–45 per cent of after-tax net income is reaching 'potential stress levels'. So, for example, if you have assets of €2m and debt of €1m, a mortgage of €1m spread over twenty years at 5 per cent interest payable monthly would set you back roughly €6,600 per month or nearly €79,000 per annum. That suggests a net income of some €175,000 is necessary.

Combining these two rules of thumb provides a good, if very conservative, guide to prudent borrowing. Of course this could be complicated significantly by the ability to source non-recourse lending and gearing within investment structures.

The rationale underlying these rules of thumb is highly relevant, particularly in an environment where we are unlikely to see rampant inflation (which had the effect of repaying debt at a much faster rate for those who had mortgages in the 1970s) and yet higher interest rates than we see at the present day. I'd suggest that every borrower should consider the impact on their finances of a 2 per cent increase in rates (more than most people anticipate but not beyond the bounds of possibility in the coming years and below the levels we had just a decade ago). A 2 per cent increase would cause the repayment in the above example to increase to roughly €7,700 per month or €93,000 per annum, bringing it to circa 53 per cent of net income and placing a much greater burden on household income.

Of course individuals will borrow more and will have capacity to borrow more than this conservative starting point but, in an environment in which

4.4 Using Debt as a Tool in your Financial Planning

rates may move northwards at some stage, be sure to check the cash flows first and make an assessment of how much increase you can afford to see in the debt-servicing costs.

Borrow More at a Higher Rate?

Frequently individuals will be tempted to borrow more at a higher rate. There's nothing particularly wrong with that but a useful tool for evaluating whether it makes sense is the concept of 'incremental borrowing cost'. Allow me to explain:

Take an individual who is planning to borrow at 80 per cent loan to value (LTV) to purchase a property at €1m. Let's assume he is going to be charged 5 per cent at 80 per cent LTV. Spread over fifteen years this would give a cost of €6,326 per month. Let's then suppose that the individual is offered a loan for 90 per cent at 5.5 per cent interest. At first glance, perhaps a worthwhile deal. The cost per month increases to €7,353, but the individual has had to put far less equity into the deal. This seems great until one looks at this in the context of 'incremental cost'. The difference in the two payments amounts to €1,027 per month to get an additional €100,000 in borrowings. What we need to do is to find a rate of interest that makes the present value of the additional repayments (€1,027) equal to €100,000 (in plain English, what it costs to borrow the extra amount plus the rest at a higher rate). Surprisingly, the answer is that the incremental cost of borrowing runs to 9.2 per cent. Therefore, for it to make sense to borrow the extra, the borrower would either have to achieve a rate of return above this level or have not found an alternative that could have done so with the €100,000 equity.

Borrow for Longer?

This issue can also be compounded when the alternative is to extend to loan term to get the loan to value higher. Using the same example as above, let's say the alternative is now to borrow at 90 per cent LTV at 5.5 per cent, this time over twenty years. Under such an arrangement the cost per month appears to reduce to €6,190. But does it?

Table 4.2 shows that to compare the true value of the two we have to compare the value of the saving of €40 per month plus the additional

165

Table 4.2: Payment Schedules for Differing Loan Terms

	Loan	Payments Yrs 1–15	Payments Yrs 15–20
5%, 15 years	€800,000	€6,326	0
5.5%, 20 years	€900,000	€6,190	€6,190
Difference	€100,000	(€136 p.m.)	€6,190 p.m.

capital of €100,000 against the present value of paying an additional €6,190 per month for five years in fifteen years time. A present value analysis suggests that the latter may in fact be less attractive.

Downside Risk and the Magnifying Effect of Borrowing

Gearing your investment will have one of two effects on the returns you can generate: it will either magnify your losses or your gains. This much may seem self-evident but it is surprising how blithely investors ignore the potential downside.

Investors who geared into the property market in Ireland in the past ten years saw the magnifying power of gearing on their original capital. Others who geared into parts of the equity market saw the pace at which their capital has eroded accelerate in the bear market years (2000–2003).

We can see this magnification effect in a simple example. Let's assume an investment of €1m financed through €250,000 equity and €750,000 in debt (with recourse to the borrower). Let's assume that the borrowing is done at 7 per cent interest, and for simplicity let's assume the rate is fixed over five years. Let's assume Asset A delivers an annual return of 12 per cent, that Asset B gains by 6 per cent, that Asset C gains 4.4 per cent per annum and Asset D loses 2 per cent per annum.

Table 4.3 shows the magnifying effect that gearing has on the end investor's returns. Figure 4.1 shows this graphically and helps to demonstrate

Table 4.3: Return on Equity Invested after 5 Years

	Return from Asset	Return on Investor's Equity
Asset A	12% p.a.	18% p.a.
Asset B	6% p.a.	4% p.a.
Asset C	4.4% p.a.	0% p.a.
Asset D	−2% p.a.	−26% p.a.

4.4 Using Debt as a Tool in your Financial Planning

Figure 4.1: The Upside and Downside of Leverage

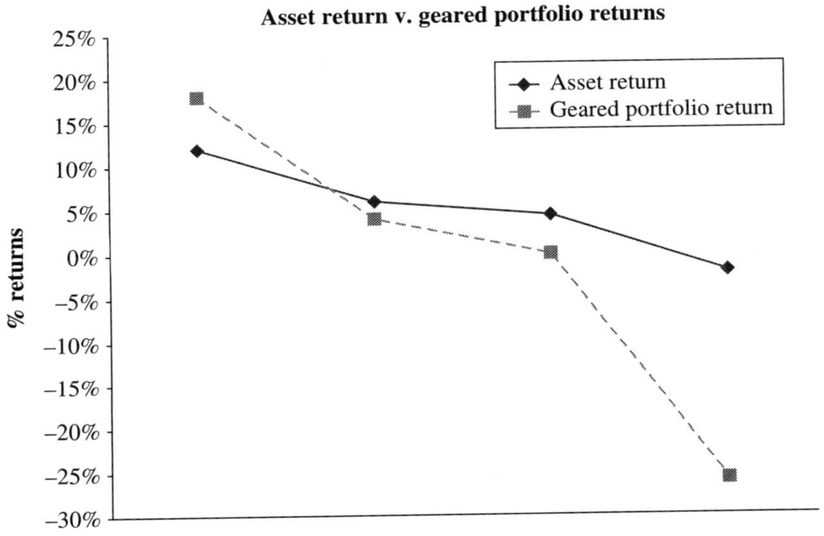

Asset return v. geared portfolio returns

Source: Kevin Quinn 2006

the significant downside that leverage entails. Only when the asset returns beat the rate of interest does the benefit of gearing begin to be felt. Anywhere below that and it is damaging. It's a simple point but one worth bearing in mind when considering how and when to deploy gearing.

This same amplification of risk/return applies in equal measure to any deal financed using non-recourse lending. What it effectively serves to do is to create a higher threshold of required return.

A further complication occurs if one gives consideration to the 'stochastic' nature of more asset returns (i.e. they don't go in a straight line). In particular when gearing into a volatile asset the losses in a down period can be dramatically exacerbated by gearing.

A Word about Advisors

The famed economist John Maynard Keynes had the following insight into the professional investor:

> Most of these [professional investors] are, in fact, largely concerned not with making superior long-term forecasts of the probable yield of an investment over its whole life but with foreseeing changes in the conventional basis of valuation a short time ahead of the public. They are concerned not with what an investment is really worth to a man who buys it 'for keeps' but with what the market will value it at under the influence of mass psychology, three months or a year hence.[1]

It is an assessment that has some merit – professional investors and advisors cannot forecast the future accurately. As you will hopefully have gleaned from this book, there are indicators and rules of thumb that we can use to evaluate the future, but we cannot hope to be accurate all the time. It is worth bearing in mind the next time you are deciding who should be guiding you through your financial choices.

There are a number of tell-tale signs that you should look for in selecting an advisor to help you execute the plans for your personal wealth. Three golden rules are worth bearing in mind:

Asset Allocation is Key

If this book has pointed to anything it's the fact that it's impossible to predict any investment market with great certainty – diversity is the only reliable tool you can use and your advisor should know this. Even if Warren Buffet famously admonished diversification as making very little sense for those who know what they are doing, the fact remains there are few Warren Buffets around.

If they don't begin by talking about asset allocation they are probably only there to sell you what's in the kit bag. It's a very bad sign if they don't believe this to be important. Neither should they oversimplify and suggest that asset allocation is 'everything'. It's not, but it is very important and is probably worth about 40 per cent of the returns you might make.

A Professional should be Uncertain and help you Understand Why

If they are too certain about what the future holds they don't have enough experience or qualifications to be advising you. Once you've seen the swings and roundabouts for a decade or two, it is a chastening and humbling experience. However a professional should have strong, well-informed opinions about markets.

While they should have the maturity to understand the unpredictable nature of markets, that should not excuse a lack of conviction about their views. If they fail to express an opinion on world markets, they don't have enough experience to be advising you.

Tax is Important

Tax is a major consideration in all wealth management plans and, while it should never be the leading part of a plan, it cannot be ignored. If they brush off tax matters as irrelevant they are under-qualified. If they put tax ahead of investments, the 'tail is wagging the dog'.

NOTES

1. (1967), *The General Theory of Employment, Interest and Money*, London: Macmillan © 1936, pp. 153–154.

Bibliography

Ahearne, Alan G., Gagnon, Joseph E., Haltmaier, Jane and Kaminm, Steven B. (2002), 'Preventing Deflation: Lessons from Japan's Experience in the 1990s', *Board of Governors of the Federal Reserve System International Finance Discussion Papers*, No. 729, June 2002, <http://www.federalreserve.gov/Pubs/ifdp/2002/729/ifdp729.pdf>, accessed 7/11/06.

Allison, Douglas T. and Lin, Felix (2004), 'Including Hedge Funds in Private Client Portfolios', *AIMR Conference Proceedings* (Feb 2004), Vol. 2004, No. 1, pp. 6–20.

Almeida Capital, *European Fundraising Review 2005*, <http://www.altassets.net/2006frreview.php>, accessed 4/11/2006.

AltAssets (2004), 'US Venture Capital Overhang Reaches $68bn', <http://www.altassets.net/news/arc/2004/nz4583.php>, accessed 04/11/2006.

Amin, Gaurav and Kat, Harry S. (2002), 'Diversification and Yield Enhancement with Hedge Funds', *Alternative Investment Research Centre: Working Paper Series No. 8*, Working Paper 1, Cass Business School, London, 7 October 2002.

Amin, Gaurav and Kat, Harry S. (2002), 'Hedge Fund Performance 1990–2000 – Do the money machines really add value?' *Alternative Investment Research Centre Working Paper Series No. 8*, Working Paper 1, 4 January 2002, Cass Business School, London.

Amin, Gaurav and Kat, Harry (2002), 'Who Should Buy Hedge Funds?' *ISMA Discussion Papers in Finance* 2002–6, ISMA Centre, University of Reading.

Arnott, Robert D. (2004), 'Managing Assets in a World of Higher Volatility and Lower Returns', *CFA Conference Proceedings: Points of Inflection – New Directions for Portfolio Management* (July 2004), Vol. 2004, No. 4, pp. 39–52.

Bibliography

Arnott, Robert D. and Bernstein, Peter L. (2002), 'What Risk Premium is "Normal"?' *Financial Analysts Journal* (March 2002), Vol. 58, No. 2, pp. 64–85.

Arnott, Robert D. and Ryan, Ronald (2001), 'The Death of the Risk Premium: Consequences of the 1990s', *Journal of Portfolio Management* (Spring), Vol. 27, No. 3, pp. 61–74.

Bishop, Matthew (2004), 'The New Kings of Capitalism: a Survey of Private Equity', *Economist*, 27 November 2004.

Brinson Partners (2002), 'Who Should Buy Hedge Funds?' *ISMA Discussion Papers in Finance 2002–6*, ISMA Centre, University of Reading, 18 March 2002.

Brueggeman, William B., Fisher, Jeffrey D. (2005), *Real Estate Finance and Investments*, 12th edition, New York: McGraw-Hill.

Campbell, John Y. and Viceira, Luis M. (2002), *Strategic Asset Allocation: Portfolio Choice for Long-Term Investors* (Clarendon Lectures in Economics 2002), Oxford: Oxford University Press.

Chun, Gregory and Shilling, James (1998), 'Real Estate Allocations and International Real Estate Markets', *Journal of Asian Real Estate Society*, Vol. 1, No. 1, pp. 17–44.

Cornell, Bradford (1999), *The Equity Risk Premium: The Long-Run Future of the Stock Market*, New York: John Wiley & Sons.

Credit Suisse First Boston/Tremont Partners LLC, 'Returns for 2006 to end June', <http://www.hedgeindex.com/hedgeindex/en/default.aspx?cy=USD>, accessed 9/11/2006.

de Tocqueville, Alexis (1986), *De la Démocratie en Amérique* I (Bouquins), France: Robert Laffont.

Dimson, Elroy, Marsh, Paul and Staunton, Mike (2002), *Triumph of the Optimists*, Princeton, New Jersey: Princeton University Press.

Bibliography

Fabozzi, Frank J. (2004), *Fixed Income Analysis for the Chartered Financial Analyst Program*, 2nd edition, Pennsylvania US: Frank J. Fabozzi Associates.

Fama, Eugene F. and French, Kenneth R. 'The Equity Premium', *Journal of Finance* (April 2002), Vol. 57, No. 2, pp. 637–659.

Glassman, J.K. and Hassett K.A. (1999), *Dow 36,000: The New Strategy for Profiting from the Coming Rise in the Stock Market*, New York: Times Books.

Glassman, J.K. and Hassett, K.A. (1998), 'Are Stocks Over-Valued? Not a Chance', *Wall Street Journal*, 20 March 1998.

Gibson, Roger C. (2000), *Asset Allocation – Balancing Financial Risk*, 3rd edition, New York: McGraw-Hill.

Graham, Benjamin and Dodd, David (1996), *Security Analysis* (the Classic 1934 Edition), US: McGraw-Hill.

Grinold, R.C. (2004), 'Closing the Gap between Expected and Possible Returns', *AIMR Conference Proceedings: Integrating Hedge Funds into a Private Wealth Strategy* (Feb 2004), Vol. 2004, No. 1, CFA Institute, pp. 33–42.

Hudson-Wilson, Susan, Fabozzi, Frank J. and Gordon, Jacques N. (2001), 'Why Real Estate', *Journal of Portfolio Management*, Vol. 28, No. 1, pp. 20–32.

International Monetary Fund (2003), 'When Bubbles Burst', *World Economic Outlook: Growth and Institutions*, April 2003, <http://www.imf.org/external/pubs/ft/weo/2003/01/pdf>, accessed 24/10/06.

Investopedia.com, 'The Florida Real Estate Craze', <http://www.investopedia.com/features/crashes/crashes4.asp>, accessed 4/11/06.

Isaac, David (2003), *Property Finance*, 2nd edition, Hampshire, UK: Palgrave Macmillan.

Ismailescu, Iuliana (2004), 'The Benefits of Commodity Investment', Centre for International Securities and Derivatives Markets, University of Massachusetts, March 2004.

Jones, Alfred (1949), 'Fashions in Forecasting', *Fortune*, March 1949, pp. 88–91, 180–186.

Jones Lang La Salle (London), 'Rising Urban Stars – Uncovering Future Winners', May 2003.

JP Morgan Asset Management, 'Real Estate – How much of their portfolio should European pensions funds allocate to real estate?' October 2005.

Keynes, John Maynard (1967), *The General Theory of Employment, Interest and Money*, London: Macmillan, pp. 153–154.

Lane, Michael F. (2001), 'Annuitization: An Eye Opening Analysis', *The Journal of Retirement Planning*, May/June 2001.

Lashinsky, Adam (2006), 'Private Equity's Barbarians are on Top – for Now', *Fortune*, 8 August 2006, <http://money.cnn.com/magazines/fortune/fortune_archive/2006/08/21/8383637/>, accessed 11/11/2006.

Lereah, David (2006), 'The Commercial Real Estate Market,' National Association of Realtors, Economic Issues and Commercial Real Estate Business Trends Forum, Washington DC, <http://www.realtor.org/Research.nsf/files/06MYMComm.pp$FILE/06MYMComm.ppt>, accessed 18/11/2006.

Malkiel, Burton G. (1996), 'How Pork Bellies Acquired an Ivy League Suit', *A Random Walk down Wall Street*, New York: W.W. Norton & Company.

Markowitz, H. (1952), 'Portfolio Selection', *Journal of Finance*, Vol. 7, March 1952, pp. 77–91.

Marshall, Chris (1991), *Life Assurance and Pensions Handbook*, 7th edition, London: Taxbriefs Limited.

Bibliography

McAllister, Patrick (2000), 'Is Direct Investment in International Property Justifiable?' *Property Management*, Vol. 18, No. 1, pp. 25–33.

Mehra, Rajnish (2001), *The Equity Risk Premium Forum Conference Proceedings* (November 2001), AIMR (now CFA Institute), pp. 60–66.

Muehring, Kevin (1996), 'John Meriwether by the Numbers: Long-term capital management results moves fund into top ranks and founder's status has grown', *Institutional Investor*, Vol. 30, No. 11, pp. 37–46.

Price Waterhouse Coopers (2005), 'Global Private Equity Report 2005', <http://www.pwcmoneytree.com/moneytree/index.jsp>, accessed 13/11/06, p.12.

Rohrer, Julie (1986), 'The Red Hot World of Julian Robertson', *Institutional Investor*, May 1986, pp. 86–92.

Ross, Stephen A. (1976), 'The Arbitrage Theory of Capital Asset Pricing', *Journal of Economic Theory*, Vol. 13, No. 3, pp. 341–360.

Rothwell, Steven (2006), 'Junk Bonds Rise in Europe', *Bloomberg News*, 3 November 2006, <http://www.iht.com/articles/2006/11/02/bloomberg/bxjunk.php>, accessed 11/11/2006.

Schiller, Robert (2005), *Irrational Exuberance*, 2nd edition, Princeton, New Jersey: Princeton University Press.

Siegel, Jeremy (2005), 'Perspectives on the Equity Risk Premium', *Bold Thinking on Investment Management*, CFA Institute, pp. 202–217.

Siegel, Jeremy (2002), *Stocks for the Long Run*, 3rd edition, UK: McGraw-Hill.

Singer, B., Staub, R. and Terhaar, K. (2002), 'Determining Appropriate Allocations to Alternative Investments', *Financial Analysts Journal*, Vol. 2002, No. 2, pp. 4–15.

Bibliography

Society of Actuaries in Ireland, (2002), 'Retirement Options and Approved Retirement Funds', 26 November 2002, <http://www.actuaries.ie/Press%20Office/Briefing%20Statements/001126-BS_Retirement%20OptionsARFs.pdf>, accessed 14/10/2006.

Thomson Financial/National Venture Capital Association (2006), *Private Equity Performance Show Stability in Q2 2006*, <http://www.nvca.org/pdf/Q206Performancefinal.pdf>, accessed 5/11/06.

INDEX

alternative assets 102, 106
annuities 131, 137–8, 139, 140–2
Approved Retirement Fund (ARF)
   see retirement
arbitrage 13, 91, 94–6, 104, 111
Arnott, Robert 26–8
asset
   allocation 3, 116, 127, 162–3, 169–70
   pools 123, 126–7
   returns 20–1, 106, 110–7, 139, 162, 166–9

bond-equity yield ratio 42
bonds
   asset-backed 66, 69–70
   bond funds 72–3, 94
   collateralised debt obligations 70
   corporate debt 66–9, 75, 112
   Euroland 74
   government bonds 21, 22, 23, 37, 67–9
   inflation-linked 21, 23, 37, 68, 116
   Japan 74
   Obligations Assimilables du Trésor (OATs) 21, 23–4, 68
   risks 71–3
   scale of markets 66–7
   semi-government 69
   strips 68
   UK gilts 72, 74, 109
   US bonds 66–7
   yield curve 23, 71–2, 95

Capital Acquisitions Tax (CAT) 127, 138, 145–54
   agricultural relief 147
   business property relief 147–8
   family business 146
   family home disposal 146
   tax-free thresholds 145
   wills 153–5
Capital Gains Tax (CGT) 124, 127–9, 130, 146, 149, 151
   dwelling house exemption 151
   qualifying assets 149–51
   retirement relief 149
   section 73 life assurance 152–3
China 29–30, 86, 113, 117
commodities 4, 14–5, 30, 43, 83–7, 97, 111–2, 114–5, 117
   indices 14, 83–4
   inflation 83–6, 112, 117
   futures 4, 14–5, 83–4, 89, 97
Commodity Trading Advisors (CTAs)
   see hedge funds
consumer 28, 30–1, 49–53, 73, 85, 112
correlation 16, 61–2, 88, 101–4, 114
costs 45, 52, 61, 65, 153, 165
currency 6, 22, 29, 53, 64–5, 95, 111, 116–7

debt 96, 162–7
Deposit Interest Retention Tax (DIRT) 124–5
derivatives 15, 83–4, 91, 96–8
diversification 60, 83, 105, 136, 169
dividends 5, 7, 25, 26, 35, 41, 64, 129, 139, 162
duration 12, 28, 71

earnings 7, 8, 32–6, 39, 41–2, 110, 132–4, 161
emerging markets 29, 31, 74, 76, 87, 91, 112
equities *see also* private equity
   Benjamin Graham 8, 36
   bubble in equity markets 6, 12, 24, 27, 30, 34, 39, 41, 52, 80

Index

equities (*cont.*)
  cult of the equity 4, 6, 116
  equity risk premium 9, 21–6, 35, 41
  Irrational Exuberance 7, 52
estate planning 125–6, 128, 147, 151, 153–4
  Approved Retirement Funds (ARF) 142
European Central Bank (ECB) 12, 37, 40, 74, 109
event-driven strategies 95

Federal Reserve Board (Fed) 12, 29–30, 37, 40, 51, 59, 73, 116
fixed income arbitrage *see* hedge funds
France 46, 68, 109, 126
fund of funds *see* hedge funds

Germany 46, 61, 109
Government, the 115–6, 124, 130
gross roll-up 104, 124–5, 127–9, 139

hedge funds 4, 12–3, 22, 43, 76, 84, 87–115, 129
  Alfred Jones 12, 89
  beta 98
  Commodity Trading Advisors (CTAs) 13, 84, 97, 101–2
  convertible arbitrage 13, 94
  distressed debt 96, 111
  equity arbitrage 94
  equity market neutral 93, 104
  fixed income arbitrage 13, 91, 95, 104
  fund of funds 91, 98, 100–1, 114
  George Soros 12, 13, 90, 94
  global macro 13, 91, 94–5
  growth of 92
  Julian Robertson 90
  long/short equity 93, 104

Long Term Capital Management (LTCM) 6, 95–6
  managed futures 4, 84, 97, 100, 114
  merger arbitrage 13, 91, 96, 104, 111
  origins 88–9
  sharpe ratio 84, 98
  shorting 4, 94–6, 101

income tax 124, 127, 129–30, 141
indices 14, 35, 62, 80, 83–4, 87, 98, 117
inflation 20–5, 27, 28–32, 34, 37–40, 41, 43, 49, 54, 72, 73, 74, 84–6, 112, 115–17, 124, 140, 164
Initial Public Offerings (IPOs) 77–8
interest rates 6, 9, 12, 20, 24, 30, 32, 34, 37, 43–8, 52–3, 57–9, 63, 66, 71, 73–5, 95, 109, 111–7, 137, 164
Internal Rate of Return (IRR) 79, 113
International Monetary Fund (IMF) 11
Internet 34, 52, 78
Ireland 21, 22, 32, 46, 51, 54, 56–7, 66, 104–5, 109–10, 113, 128, 131, 137–8, 142, 152, 160, 166
Italy 67

Japan 20, 29, 30, 44, 55–6, 74

life assurance 128, 133, 137, 152, 155–62
  co-directors 158–9
  corporate shareholder protection 159
  Keyman 159–60
  'life of another' 156–7, 159
  'own life in trust' 157–8, 159
  partnership assurance 156
  personal shareholder protection 159
Liquidity
  bonds 72
  commodities 87

180

Index

Liquidity (*cont.*)
  global economy 29, 40, 46, 59
  hedge funds 105
  pensions 136
  private equity 76–7
  property 61–2
Luxembourg 128

Markowitz, Harry 3, 15–6
monetarism 20
mortgage-backed securities 66–7
mutual funds 13, 34, 92–3

net funds 124, 128, 139, 141

offshore funds 105, 129
options markets 15, 83, 97

pension funds 6, 58, 92, 115, 124, 130, 134
performance (asset class) 106, 109–10, 113, 130
permanent health insurance 160–61
Private equity 4, 13–4, 43, 76–87, 101, 106, 109, 111, 114–5
  buy-out 14, 76–80
  J-Curves 79–80, 82
  mezzanine 76
  US private equity performance 78, 81
  venture capital 76
property (*also* 'real estate') 3, 4, 7, 8–12, 19–20, 22, 24, 30, 32, 39, 43–66, 110–1, 113–7, 128, 132, 134–6, 146–54, 165–6
  Asia 64–5
  bubbles 11, 50–1
  commercial market 48, 52, 56–7, 65, 111, 113

Ireland 10, 51, 56–64, 110, 113
Japan 55–6
UK Commercial 44–8
UK Residential 48–9, 113
US Commercial 52–5, 111
US residential 49–52
yield gap 32, 44, 46–7, 59, 63–65

Retirement 11, 30, 34, 123–42, 149, 154–5, 158, 160, 163
  Additional Voluntary Contribution (AVC) 131, 136–7
  annuities 130–1, 137, 139–42
  Approved Retirement Fund (ARF) 125, 137–142
  contribution rates 134
  eligible earnings 132
  executive pensions 131, 133–4, 137
  pension reserve fund 131
  personal pensions 130–42
  Personal Retirement Savings Account (PRSA) 131, 133, 136–7
  situation on death 141
  Small Self-Administered Pension (SSAP) 131, 134–7

serious illness cover 160–1

taxation 57, 104, 127–130, 159
  of company investments 129

unit funds 104, 132, 134
unit trusts 45–6, 92, 128, 136

venture capital *see* private equity
vintage year 79
volatility 4, 27, 29, 36, 62, 64, 75, 84, 94, 101, 111